TWO GOOD ROUNDS
SUPERSTARS

TWO GOOD ROUNDS
SUPERSTARS
Golf Stories from the World's Greatest Athletes

BY ELISA GAUDET

SKYHORSE PUBLISHING

Pam
Thanks for all
your support!
Enjoy

Cheers!
Elisa

Skyhorse Publishing books may be purchased in bulk at special discounts for sales promotion, corporate gifts, fund-raising, or educational purposes. Special editions can also be created to specifications. For details, contact the Special Sales Department, Sports Publishing, 307 West 36th Street, 11th Floor, New York, NY 10018 or info@skyhorsepublishing.com.

Skyhorse® and Skyhorse Publishing® are registered trademarks of Skyhorse Publishing, Inc.®, a Delaware corporation.

Visit our website at www.skyhorsepublishing.com.

10 9 8 7 6 5 4 3 2 1

Library of Congress Cataloging-in-Publication Data is available on file.

ISBN: 978-1-62914-214-2

Printed in China

Sports icons courtesy of Thinkstock

Logo designed by Matt Curtis of Curtis Illustration

To the professional athletes who inspire us all to achieve and
strive to be the best in everything we do.

The millions of golf fans around the world who love and
appreciate this beautiful game.

&

Paul Bader
For your love and support.

"It took me seventeen years to get three thousand hits in baseball. I did it in one afternoon on the golf course."

— Hank Aaron

"Some people want it to happen, some wish it would happen, others make it happen."

— Michael Jordan

"Do your best, one shot at a time, and then move on."

— Nancy Lopez

"If my mind can conceive it, and my heart can believe it—then I can achieve it."

— Muhammad Ali

Contents

© Bill Menzel

Foreword

As a sportsman and sports fan, it's a pleasure to contribute to this book by Elisa Gaudet, a follow-up for her previous title *Two Good Rounds: 19th Hole Stories from the World's Greatest Golfers*. With this latest book she's onto a home run, slam dunk, ace, knockout, or whatever sporting term of excellence you can think of.

When I was growing up, I loved playing all sports—especially golf, tennis, cricket, and rugby. These days I enjoy watching almost any top-class sport either on television or, when my schedule allows, live. Sports at the highest level have always fascinated me and, like any keen sports fan, I'm interested in the characters who make it to the top of their chosen discipline.

That's the core appeal of *Golf Stories from the World's Greatest Athletes*. Elisa has managed to secure interviews with fifty-four of the world's elite athletes from a range of different sports—stars from the worlds of NFL, NBA, NHL, MLB, boxing, NASCAR, soccer, surfing, Rugby Union, Formula One, and tennis, plus some Olympic gold medal winners.

Each athlete answers a series of questions that gets to the heart of why he or she loves the game of golf. It's a fun, feel-good, respectful, lighthearted look at golf and the players' lives and personalities, and it shows just how popular golf is with elite athletes and the enjoyment they receive from spending time playing.

For anyone reading this book, there will obviously be names that jump out, all-time heroes, and personal favorites. That was the case with me. I also came across a few guys I've played golf with in the past and others I didn't know so well but enjoyed reading about. That variety is part of the book's appeal.

Each athlete's chosen charity is also featured, which is a worthwhile acknowledgement of work done mostly behind the scenes. I can speak for all professional athletes when I say we're lucky to do what we do, and we all share a passion for giving back. For me, it's why we established the Els for Autism Foundation and the Ernie Els & Fancourt Foundation. Giving people the tools and opportunities to enjoy a better life is the ultimate and, as I'm sure any athlete would agree, means more than any trophy or gold medal.

I really enjoyed reading this book. I think you will, too.

—Ernie Els
Four-time major champion and a major sports fan

Introduction

The influence of sports and athletes in our lives is enormous. One of the most incredible things about sports is their ability to transcend language, borders, politics, religion, sex, and race. Identifying a new way to capture this transcendent quality was my goal in writing this book.

In a continuation of the *Two Good Rounds* spirit, this book is a tribute to great athletes around the globe and their passion for golf. Golf is an international sport that continues to expand into more countries than ever before. As many have noted, no matter how good you are at a certain sport, golf is the great equalizer. This is especially true for the athletes interviewed in this book who have excelled to the highest levels of their chosen sport. While golf has, at times, humbled and challenged them, it has also reignited their competitive flames. They have all found great satisfaction in playing the game of golf. I felt it was important to identify a truly diverse group of athletes worldwide who have two things in common; they excelled at the highest level in their sport and have a passion for the game of golf. Also, it was important to highlight the diversity of sports represented and bring attention to ones that are not as well known in the United States. Athletes from around the globe representing an array of sports participated, including: cricket, soccer, baseball, football, swimming, tennis, hockey, basketball, skiing, surfing, boxing, rowing, skating, rugby, NASCAR, Formula One, and bullfighting. No matter the athlete's size or skill level, whether a 5'3" horse jockey or a 6'6" NBA star, golf remains the great equalizer.

Golf has the ability to excite, inspire, and unite people. One of the powerful ways in which this attribute manifests itself is in the many charity golf outings held to raise money and awareness for great causes. Every athlete in this book has participated in these competitions and lent his or her image and talent to enhance an event. Many athletes have their own charities and, as a part of their fundraising efforts, hold golf tournaments. An important component in this book was to ensure that the athletes' own charities or those they support are highlighted and recognized.

A common theme that came up through the interviews was the importance of believing in yourself even when others don't. There will always be failure—missed shots, lost games, and missed cuts—but every athlete acknowledged this was part of the process. The ability to get up, keep going, and not let failure define them was a key factor in moving forward and achieving success. One of the things I found remarkable was how many great athletes truly understand that they learn more in their failure than in moments of success and how important self-awareness is in getting them to the next level. It is interesting how this lifelong series of ups and downs can be experienced in a single round of golf.

Sports have always been a mirror for life, and the inspiration and dedication we gain from watching our favorite sports heroes motivates us to reach higher levels in our professional and personal lives. Often we follow and see the athletes we admire when they are at the height of their career and winning. We do not see the hours they spend in the gym or the time spent after a loss. It is my hope that this collection of stories about elite athletes who have found a passion for golf will inspire each of you to dream big, reach far, live your truth, and know that when you fail there is always a way to get up. Truly go for it in sports and life knowing that to dare is to do and to fear is to fail. With golf, as with life, there is always another shot. How you play the next one is the question. Dream big, play and live with passion, and enjoy the ride.

TWO GOOD ROUNDS
SUPERSTARS

Michael Phelps
SWIMMING

Michael Phelps, an American swimmer, is the most decorated Olympian of all time, having tallied a total of twenty-two medals. Phelps also holds the all-time record for Olympic gold medals, with eighteen. Phelps took the record for the most first-place finishes at any single Olympic Games when he won eight gold medals in 2008.

HANDICAP

The max, ha-ha.

FIRST INTRODUCTION TO GOLF

I played a little bit with my friends, but because of my intense swimming schedule, I never had time to concentrate on golf. In 2010, I did travel to China and had my first lesson from Hank Haney at Mission Hills; it was then that I realized how much work my golf game needed! Golf is one of the most humbling games I've tried to do in my entire life.

FAVORITE COURSE(S)

I've been really lucky to play so many incredible courses while filming *The Haney Project*—courses in China, Cabo, the Bahamas, etc. My favorite so far is the Old Course and Kingsbarns Golf Links in Scotland.

BEST GOLF MEMORIES

I'll never forget playing in the Pro-Am at the Ryder Cup; there were so many people there watching and everyone was cheering loudly. It was so cool to see spectators dressed in red, white, and blue, and some children were even wearing swim caps while watching me play. The Ryder Cup creates such a unique environment; it's really hard to beat.

I also played in the Phoenix Open Pro-Am with Bubba Watson, and I've never been so nervous as I was playing the 16th hole with that many people watching. When I walked up, everyone starting chanting U-S-A, which was very memorable!

My most memorable golf shot was when I sunk a 159-foot putt at Kingsbarns, recording the longest-ever televised putt. That was crazy—obviously one of the biggest highlights of my golfing experience. I wasn't expecting it to go in when I hit, I was just trying to get it up close to the pin so I'd have a makeable birdie putt. As the ball was making its way toward the hole, I could see that it was on a good line, had good speed, and as it got closer and closer I started thinking it might have a chance. And when it did, it was a total rush, as you can probably tell from my reaction with the fist pump. I'm hopeful that there will be many more great shots in my future!

HOW DOES GOLF COMPARE TO SWIMMING

I'm not sure how much swimming helps with golf; in golf, you're trying to stay out of the water! However, I am a very competitive person, and I think that helps in everything I do. I like to think that I have a pretty good mental approach to things, which was a big factor in my success in the pool. Now I am trying to apply that same attitude toward golf.

TWO GOOD ROUNDS SUPERSTARS

Just one? While filming *The Haney Project*, Hank gave me so much insight and knowledge about the game and the mechanics of a good swing. One area I have been working on is swinging the club faster and making sure I swing all the way through the ball. I've had a tendency to slow down after hitting the ball, so I am working on my follow-through to make sure I complete my swing.

ONE GOLF TIP

I always tell people to "Dream, Plan, Reach." It's important to come up with a dream and a plan for how you're going to reach it. It's important that children know anything is possible!

ONE LIFE TIP

The Michael Phelps Foundation hosts an annual golf classic, which is the largest annual fund-raising event for my foundation's programs (www.michaelphelpsfoundation.org). It's always a memorable weekend and raises awareness and funds to support the Foundation's mission of promoting healthy and active lives, especially for children, primarily by expanding their opportunities in the sport of swimming.

FAVORITE CHARITY GOLF EVENTS

For the season finale of *The Haney Project*, I got to play with Olympic legends; Mike Eruzione, Sugar Ray Leonard, Bruce Jenner, and Seth Wescott . . . what a memorable day! And of course, who doesn't have Michael Jordan in their dream foursome?

DREAM FOURSOME

A cold beer.

FAVORITE 19TH HOLE DRINK

Anyone who has played at El Dorado knows that the comfort stations are impossible to beat . . . no need to wait until the end to enjoy food and drinks!

FAVORITE COUNTRY CLUB GRILL ROOM / 19TH HOLE

I have never gotten a hole in one . . . but I hope to soon!

HOLE IN ONE

MICHAEL PHELPS

Harrah's HARVEYS	
JORDAN	3 ?
RICE	3 4
ALLEN R	2 5

Courtesy of Tahoecelebritygolf.com

Ray Allen
BASKETBALL

Ray Allen currently plays for the Miami Heat. The ten-time NBA All-Star previously played for three other teams and has won two NBA championships. He was also a member of the 2000 US Men's Basketball Team, which won the Olympic gold medal.

HANDICAP

To a scratch golfer, 1.9.

FIRST INTRODUTION TO GOLF

I was first introduced to golf in college. I was the "Man on Campus," and I was pretty good at a lot of things. A buddy said to me, "I don't think you can play golf. You couldn't even get the ball in the air." It was a challenge and I went out there, and once I hit a good shot that was it; I was hooked. Every summer I would play in every golf tournament I could and play my own ball.

FAVORITE COURSE(S)

Augusta National and Whistling Straights.

BEST GOLF MEMORIES

Two summers ago, I went to Ireland on a golfing trip and it was very exciting and very memorable. I really like the courses and the atmosphere. Ballybunion, Doonbeg, and Lahinch were a few of my favorites.

HOW DOES GOLF COMPARE TO BASKETBALL

I used to stand over my wedge shot and just swing at the ball and hope for the best shot. The same in basketball, I was guessing. Then I just started working on everything that I may do in a game, every shot. Chances of execution are stronger if I have practiced all the possible shots. Now when I have a tee time I get to the range an hour before and use all the clubs and the wedge and hit every shot that may happen before I play. The same in basketball. Golf definitely helped my basketball.

ONE GOLF TIP

Hit shots on the course as if you always have to leave the next shot for your partner.

ONE LIFE TIP

What determines your success is how you handle adversity.

FAVORITE CHARITY GOLF EVENTS

Ray of Hope Foundation hosts the Ray Allen Golf Tournament, held at the TPC River Highlands in Cromwell, Connecticut (www.ray34.com/about-ray/activist). I started the foundation in 1997; it assists with sports-related and community-based programs and provides avenues of opportunity through which our youth can hope to realize their full potential.

DREAM FOURSOME

Tiger Woods, Michael Jordan, and Charles Barkley for comic relief.

FAVORITE 19TH HOLE DRINK

Ice Tea (Non-alcoholic Long Island Ice Tea).

FAVORITE COUNTRY CLUB GRILL ROOM / 19TH HOLE

Shelter Harbor Golf Club in Rhode Island and Old Sandwich Golf Club in Plymouth, Massachusetts.

I have had three holes in one.

One summer I was golfing at Everett Golf & Country Club in Seattle and a journalist was doing a story on golf and basketball, so they were walking some of the holes with me and a buddy. We were on the 7th hole and the journalist and photographer were following and the editor was in front of us and waved us through. I hit my shot. It was 190 yards uphill. I used a 7-iron and it went in the hole. By the time the round was over, everyone knew I had gotten a hole in one; the word had spread around the club. Remember that commercial where the guy gets the hole in one and no one is around? Well this was the opposite.

The same buddy, James Collins, was with me when I got the second hole in one. He just said, "No way; this is not for real."

© AP Photo/Wilfredo Lee

© Bill Menzel

Andy Roddick
TENNIS

Andy Roddick is a professional tennis player. Previously ranked number one in the world, he won the 2003 US Open.

Five.

HANDICAP

One year after Wimbledon there was a week of rain. I usually go out on the boat on sunny days, but the lake had overflowed so we went out and played golf at the Lions Municipal Golf Course in Austin, Texas. That was the beginning of the addiction.

FIRST INTRODUCTION TO GOLF

Pine Valley Golf Club—I love it—and Wade Hampton Golf Club in North Carolina.

FAVORITE COURSE(S)

My best golfing experience was when I caddied for Zach Johnson in 2011 at the Masters Par 3 competition. I was nervous because I did not want to mess up or give him the wrong clubs. I didn't even think that he would only need a few clubs because it is all par 3. He came with the full tournament bag with all the clubs, and I had to carry the heavy bag the whole time. Also, when I played Pebble Beach I was walking and playing by myself—just me and the caddy,

BEST GOLF MEMORIES

no one else on the course. It was my first experience at Pebble and the best.

HOW DOES GOLF COMPARE TO TENNIS	There are some parallels, as with any sport. In tennis you can miss shots and still win; not in golf. Mentally, golf is extremely difficult. In golf you can get an unlucky bounce like Phil at the Masters, and it can change a lot.
ONE GOLF TIP	Don't take golf tips from me.
ONE LIFE TIP	That would require me having figured things out.
FAVORITE CHARITY GOLF EVENTS	The Pebble Beach Pro-Am—I was like a kid in a candy store when I got the invite.
	I have a foundation, the Andy Roddick Foundation, that focuses on empowering youth in our communities (www.arfoundation.org). ARF believes talent is universal but opportunity is not. We started having a golf tournament as a fund-raiser, the ARF Celebrity Golf Classic.
DREAM FOURSOME	Jack Nicklaus, Arnold Palmer, Michael Jordan, and Alister MacKenzie.
FAVORITE 19TH HOLE DRINK	In Austin, where I play, I am usually the first out. I like to play early, so the Bloody Mary is my drink.

Seminole Golf Club has the best locker room that ever existed. It is really incredible, very big, and it has so much history and tradition.

FAVORITE
COUNTRY CLUB
GRILL ROOM /
19TH HOLE

No. Not yet, but I play with a group of friends at Spanish Oaks, and we have a deal that whoever makes a hole in one, we all have to get together and go to Vegas that night. No excuses.

HOLE IN ONE

© Getty Images

Wayne Gretzky
ICE HOCKEY

Wayne Gretzky is a former professional Canadian ice hockey star who played with four teams over the course of his twenty-year tenure in the NHL. He is the NHL career point leader. He won four Stanley Cups and was inducted into the Hockey Hall of Fame in 1999.

Twelve.

HANDICAP

I was about 15 years old, and my uncle had an extra set of golf clubs. I went with my best friend John Mowat to the Brantford municipal golf courses in Ontario; we paid fifteen dollars to play.

FIRST INTRODUCTION TO GOLF

My favorite course is Sherwood Country Club, where I live, and the Double Eagle Club in Ohio.

FAVORITE COURSE(S)

Playing with Michael Barnett, who was my manager for thirty years, Mark McCormack, and Arnold Palmer the year after he retired. I played Augusta National two times. I have a friend who I played in a member–guest with ten years ago; he knows Augusta National.

BEST GOLF MEMORIES

I was watching the Masters on TV when Mike Weir, a fellow Canadian, won and this guy got my call through to Butler Cabin, which is pretty impressive, to congratulate Mike Weir. It was a great win.

HOW DOES GOLF COMPARE TO HOCKEY

It does not, except for being competitive and the thrill of being successful. Hockey is high speed, high level, and golf is slow and mechanical.

ONE GOLF TIP

Enjoy the game, especially as amateurs.

ONE LIFE TIP

Respect. No matter how good or nice you are, someone is nicer. I try to instill that with my kids.

FAVORITE CHARITY GOLF EVENTS

Michael Jordan's tournament is great, and he is a great golf partner (www.mjcigolf.com). I also have fun with Ahmad Rashad at his event (www.ahmadrashadcelebrityclassic.com).

DREAM FOURSOME

My dad, Babe Ruth, Gordie Howe. I have a scorecard from the Rye Country Club signed by Babe Ruth from 1937.

FAVORITE 19TH HOLE DRINK

Molson Canadian. I got involved in winemaking, and a few years ago we partnered with John Peller for the wine business and to expand the Wayne Gretzky Estate Winery (www.gretzkyestateswines.com). It is a family business for both of us. There is a No. 99 series of wines.

The Edmonton Country Club in Canada because it feels like home. FAVORITE
COUNTRY CLUB
GRILL ROOM /
19TH HOLE

No.   HOLE IN ONE

© AP Photo/Jim Rogash

WAYNE GRETZKY

© Bill Menzel

Michael Strahan
FOOTBALL

Michael Strahan is a former NFL defensive end who spent all fourteen seasons of his career playing for the New York Giants. Strahan holds the record for the most sacks in one season.

Strahan has appeared in TV commercials for Sports Authority and Right Guard Antiperspirant as a golfer.

FUN GOLF FACT

Golf is my handicap. When I was playing more, I was about a ten.

HANDICAP

I kept getting invited to celebrity golf tournaments and turning them down because I did not know how to play and I felt embarrassed. Finally, I went out on the range and got comfortable with it.

FIRST INTRODUCTION TO GOLF

Hamilton Farm Golf Club and Winged Foot Golf Club.

FAVORITE COURSE(S)

My best memory is golfing with Bill Clinton.

BEST GOLF MEMORIES

HOW DOES GOLF COMPARE TO FOOTBALL	They are similar in that you have to forget about the bad shot or bad play and not let it get to you. You cannot let the past affect you.
ONE GOLF TIP	Keep your head down.
ONE LIFE TIP	Don't stand in front of someone hitting a golf ball.
FAVORITE CHARITY GOLF EVENTS	I host my own golf tournament and now play in a number of charity golf events.
DREAM FOURSOME	Dad, if I can convince him to play; my fiancée Nicole, so I don't need to rush to get home; and God, because I need him the way I hit.
FAVORITE 19TH HOLE DRINK	Arnold Palmer, and sometimes I like it with a little kick (John Daly).
FAVORITE COUNTRY CLUB GRILL ROOM / 19TH HOLE	Hamilton Farms—it is my home course and I like the pool and to just chill there.
HOLE IN ONE	No.

MICHAEL STRAHAN

Courtesy of Dale Jarrett

Dale Jarrett
NASCAR

Dale Jarrett is a former American race car driver and current sports commentator known for winning the 1999 NASCAR Winston Cup Series championship. He is the son of two-time Grand National Champion Ned Jarrett.

Seven.

HANDICAP

My dad taught me. I started when I was 9. It was the 1960s and they did not have junior golf clubs, so my dad made clubs by cutting them down. We would play at Camden Country Club in Camden, South Carolina. My mom is 81 and still plays golf, and my dad is 87 and still plays.

FIRST INTRODUCTION TO GOLF

Augusta National and Pebble Beach.

FAVORITE COURSE(S)

Playing with my family—with my mom, dad, and brother.

BEST GOLF MEMORIES

Also playing with Arnold Palmer at the 1999 Vantage Championship at Tanglewood Park in Clemmons, North Carolina.

HOW DOES GOLF COMPARE TO NASCAR	Patience does help you get to the end in racing; it is the same as in golf. Also temperament, physical condition, and hand-eye coordination are important in both sports. Golf helped me in racing as a sport and in driving. I was able to play with customers and spend time with them away from the track.
ONE GOLF TIP	Work on your short game.
ONE LIFE TIP	Treat others the way you want to be treated.
FAVORITE CHARITY GOLF EVENTS	Cancer research is important to my family. We have held the Ned Jarrett American Cancer Society Golf Classic for twenty-seven years.
DREAM FOURSOME	Arnold Palmer, Jack Nicklaus, Tiger Woods.
FAVORITE 19TH HOLE DRINK	Michelob Ultra—I usually try to get one quickly.
FAVORITE COUNTRY CLUB GRILL ROOM / 19TH HOLE	Catawba Country Club in Newton, North Carolina and Whisper Rock in Scottsdale, Arizona.
HOLE IN ONE	Six. Perhaps the best was the hole in one I made at my father's tournament for cancer. I did not have to buy drinks because we had an alcohol sponsor at the event.

DALE JARRETT

Courtesy of Tahoecelebritygolf.com

Brandi Chastain
SOCCER

Brandi Chastain plays for the California Storm of the Women's Premier Soccer League. She previously played on the US Women's National Soccer Team. In the 1999 FIFA Women's World Cup final, she kicked the game-winning penalty kick.

My handicap is my golf game; fourteen.

HANDICAP

My grandfather first introduced me to golf when I was around 8 years old. He would take me to the Bing Crosby Tournament and tell me all kinds of stories about Jack Nicklaus and Arnold Palmer, and we would have lunch at the driving range.

FIRST INTRODUCTION TO GOLF

My favorites are the San Jose Country Club, the Monterey Peninsula Country Club, and Pebble Beach.

FAVORITE COURSE(S)

My best memories golfing are the times I spent with my grandfather and playing with my husband. At the AT&T, I had a great drive off the tee. I was sixty yards from the green, and I shanked it into the dirt. I was in a bunker and from there hit it right in the hole. It

BEST GOLF MEMORIES

was great—with all the people there, I got right in the sand bunker and did a sand angel.

HOW DOES GOLF COMPARE TO SOCCER

Soccer and golf are similar in the ball flight, so I definitely understand the concept in both and how to do a high or low fade or a draw. So I get the ball concept. With both sports you need to be in the moment, while soccer does have a wider aperture. The times where I have a free kick or penalty kick, it is more like golf with the ball being static and having to implement the techniques learned.

ONE GOLF TIP

My best tip is from Johnny Miller—finish down with your head behind the ball.

ONE LIFE TIP

Life is too short—ENJOY!

FAVORITE CHARITY GOLF EVENTS

It is a tie between the Michael Jordan and the American Century Championship; both of them are great (www.mjcigolf.com and www.tahoecelebritygolf.com).

I have my own foundation to help young girls, the Reach Up Foundation, and I support the Bay Area Woman's Sports Initiative (www.reachupworld.com and www.bawsi.org).

DREAM FOURSOME

My husband, dad, and grandfather.

FAVORITE 19TH HOLE DRINK

Water.

The Michael Jordan Tournament used to be in the Bahamas, and I always loved the grill room there at the One&Only. Looking over the blue ocean, it is very beautiful.

No.

FAVORITE COUNTRY CLUB GRILL ROOM / 19TH HOLE

HOLE IN ONE

© AP Photo/Rusty Kennedy

Courtesy of Tahoecelebritygolf.com

Kelly Slater
SURFING

Kelly Slater is an American professional surfer and eleven-time ASP World Champion. He is the most successful champion in surfing history.

Three.

HANDICAP

I played golf with a friend when I was 23 and got hooked after a few shots. Spessard Holland Golf Course in Melbourne Beach, Florida.

FIRST INTRODUCTION TO GOLF

St. Andrews and Los Angeles Country Club North.

FAVORITE COURSE(S)

My favorite memories are getting a double eagle in Japan and when a friend got a hole in one. He is Australian and he bought drinks.

BEST GOLF MEMORIES

HOW DOES GOLF COMPARE TO SURFING	The two are similar in that you need to completely focus for hours, and you are in a competition. In both sports you have to think about a technique. One difference is in surfing there is no formal learning, and you figure it out yourself. In golf there are lots of lessons and specific techniques.
ONE GOLF TIP	Don't let the club pass your hands before you hit the ball.
ONE LIFE TIP	Relax.
FAVORITE CHARITY GOLF EVENTS	I really like the AT&T Pebble Beach Pro-Am (www.attpbgolf.com).
DREAM FOURSOME	Freddy Couples, Adam Scott, and my younger brother.
FAVORITE 19TH HOLE DRINK	Juices—any fresh squeezed juices. I don't really drink.
FAVORITE COUNTRY CLUB GRILL ROOM / 19TH HOLE	The bar on the 17th hole at St. Andrews. The burgers are amazing, and when I was there it was very cool because I walked in and there was Ernie Els.
HOLE IN ONE	Yes, one on a par 3 in Beverly Hills, Los Angeles. It was on this eighteen-hole par 3 course, and it is like two dollars to play.

KELLY SLATER

33

Jerry Bailey
THOROUGHBRED JOCKEY

Jerry Bailey is a retired American Hall of Fame thoroughbred racing jockey with 5,892 wins.

Five.

HANDICAP

My father played golf; he was a scratch golfer and the club champion in El Paso, Texas. When I was 8 years old, I would shag balls for him. Also a very good friend, a builder on Long Island, took me out. I shot a 121. I didn't think about horse racing and it completely took my mind off work. I loved it. Golf grabbed me quickly, and I joined three clubs—one in Long Island, one in Saratoga, and one in Florida.

FIRST INTRODUCTION TO GOLF

My favorites are Augusta National, where I stayed on property and it was awesome, and Indian Creek Country Club in Florida.

FAVORITE COURSE(S)

Perhaps when I holed out for an eagle and when I shot even par at Saratoga National.

BEST GOLF MEMORIES

HOW DOES GOLF COMPARE TO HORSE RACING	They both challenge me and are competitive. Racing is about fifths of a second and very fast. Golf is challenging but very slow; it slows the mind down. I put a lot of thought into how it will unfold.
ONE GOLF TIP	Slow down and slow your swing down.
ONE LIFE TIP	Enjoy the moment.
FAVORITE CHARITY GOLF EVENTS	Eclipse Charity Golf Tournament is a great event I host to support the Permanently Disabled Jockeys Fund and the Thoroughbred Retirement Foundation, which provides aftercare and adoptive services for retired racehorses (www.pdjf.org and www.trfinc .org).
DREAM FOURSOME	Arnold Palmer, Gary Player, and Charles Barkley.
FAVORITE 19TH HOLE DRINK	Cranberry juice, club soda, and lime.
FAVORITE COUNTRY CLUB GRILL ROOM / 19TH HOLE	Adios Golf Club in Florida—the locker room and grill room.
HOLE IN ONE	No, not even close.

JERRY BAILEY

Steve Waugh
CRICKET

Steve Waugh was captain of the Australian Test Cricket Team from 1999 to 2004, led Australia to fifteen of their record sixteen consecutive Test wins, led the 1999 Cricket World Cup team, and was inducted into the ICC Cricket Hall of Fame in January 2010.

HANDICAP

Eight.

FIRST INTRODUCTION TO GOLF

I started to play when I was 18 years old through some high school friends. I played cricket and semipro football, and it is a natural progression to play golf when in sports. Many of the cricket guys play golf in the off-season.

FAVORITE COURSE(S)

St. Andrews—I really enjoy the tradition, that it is a unique and special place, and you have to earn every shot.

New South Wales in Sydney—it is a challenging course that tests your skills. New South Wales Golf Club is a golf course designed by Alister MacKenzie in 1926.

BEST GOLF MEMORIES

I really enjoy playing in the Dunhill Links and playing with the pro golfers. Twenty teams play the last days with the professional golfers, and it is a real adrenaline rush, the thrill of playing professional sports.

HOW DOES GOLF COMPARE TO CRICKET

You have a lot of time between shots to talk yourself out of shots. They are both mentally challenging; you have to be mentally strong. In golf the ball is stationary; in cricket it is moving, but both involve technique, patience, and the ability to overcome adversity. You have to be able to get out of bad shots and boost yourself up.

ONE GOLF TIP

Slow your swing down and swing at 80 percent pace.

ONE LIFE TIP

Overcoming adversity and coming back. How you come back from adversity shows your true colors and character.

FAVORITE CHARITY GOLF EVENTS

To me, being an Australian is about looking after your mates, taking care of the less fortunate, supporting the underdog, and enhancing the spirit that makes all Australians unique. My foundation does a number of events to raise funds (www.stevewaughfoundation.com.au).

DREAM FOURSOME

Mother Teresa, Nelson Mandela, David Attenborough, and Harry Houdini. This would truly be about the quality of the companionship more than the quality of golf.

FAVORITE 19TH HOLE DRINK

Arnold Palmer and Coke.

The bar at New South Wales Golf Club for a quick stop; then I am back to domestic duties—I have three kids.

FAVORITE COUNTRY CLUB GRILL ROOM / 19TH HOLE

No, and I have been frustratingly close. I think is this going to be the shot that gets me a hole in one. I want one.

HOLE IN ONE

© AP Photo/Mark Baker

Courtesy of Tahoecelebritygolf.com

John Smoltz
BASEBALL

John Smoltz is a retired MLB pitcher and current sportscaster. Smoltz played for more than twenty years with the Atlanta Braves. The Cy Young Award winner was voted into the All-Star team eight times and is part of the 3,000 Strikeouts Club.

Two.	**HANDICAP**
An old buddy from high school took me to play a nine-hole course in Lansing, Michigan when I was 20. I had time on my hands and started playing. I fell in love with golf and want to be as good as I can. I have been working on that for the past five years.	**FIRST INTRODUCTION TO GOLF**
Hawks Ridge Golf Club and the Golf Club of Georgia.	**FAVORITE COURSE(S)**
Two of my best golfing memories are playing with Tiger Woods at Augusta National three weeks before the Masters and when I shot a 63 at the Floridian in Florida.	**BEST GOLF MEMORIES**

HOW DOES GOLF COMPARE TO BASEBALL	Two similarities are that you are looking at a target and the mental aspect. Guys can pick you up in baseball, but not in golf. If you think negatively, then negative things happen.
ONE GOLF TIP	Try not to move. Stay centered.
ONE LIFE TIP	Don't be afraid to fail.
FAVORITE CHARITY GOLF EVENTS	Tahoe American Century, Children's Healthcare of Atlanta, and Kings Ridge Christian School in Alpharetta, Georgia (www .tahoecelebritygolf.com, www.choa.org, and www.kingsridgecs .org).
DREAM FOURSOME	I like to laugh, so it would be Bill Cosby, Bill Murray, and Jim Carey.
FAVORITE 19TH HOLE DRINK	Arnold Palmer.
FAVORITE COUNTRY CLUB GRILL ROOM / 19TH HOLE	The Hawks Ridge Clubhouse.
HOLE IN ONE	I have had seven, and the best was on the 11th hole, a par 4, at Shadow Creek.

JOHN SMOLTZ

Oscar De La Hoya
BOXING

Oscar De La Hoya is a professional boxer who won a gold medal at the Barcelona Olympic Games. He has garnered ten world titles.

Six.

HANDICAP

My brother first introduced me to golf when I was 27, and he is also the one who introduced me to boxing.

FIRST INTRODUCTION TO GOLF

Lakeside Golf Club in California.

FAVORITE COURSE(S)

My best golfing memory is my first hole in one. It was at Friendly Hills Country Club on hole number eight, 187 yards downhill. It was the best feeling.

BEST GOLF MEMORIES

HOW DOES GOLF COMPARE TO BOXING

They are very different sports, but what they have in common for me is the rush you feel when you make a good shot or land a left hook—the adrenaline rush.

ONE GOLF TIP

Finish your swing.

ONE LIFE TIP

When you fall, make sure you know you can get back up. Fight hard.

FAVORITE CHARITY GOLF EVENTS

The AT&T at Pebble Beach is amazing. It is intense, fun, and serious golf (www.attpbgolf.com/charity). It is a lot more pressure playing with PGA Tour pros, but I love the feeling of trying my best and doing my best on the big stage. Also, my foundation, the Oscar de la Hoya Foundation. I have an annual golf tournament, the Oscar De La Hoya's Annual Celebrity Golf Classic (www.goldenboypromotions.com).

DREAM FOURSOME

Phil Mickelson, Ben Hogan, and my wife.

FAVORITE 19TH HOLE DRINK

Pellegrino on the rocks with a lime.

FAVORITE COUNTRY CLUB GRILL ROOM / 19TH HOLE

My favorite is the Tap Room at Pebble Beach.

HOLE IN ONE

I have had two; Friendly Hills on the 8th hole and Angeles National Golf Club on the 12th hole, 130 yards. I used a pitching wedge.

OSCAR DE LA HOYA

Courtesy of Tahoecelebritygolf.com

Charles Barkley
BASKETBALL

Charles Barkley is a retired professional basketball player known for his dominance as a power forward. He played with the Philadelphia 76ers, Phoenix Suns, and Houston Rockets. He was a five-time All-NBA First Team selection. Barkley was inducted into the Naismith Memorial Basketball Hall of Fame in 2006.

I don't have one.

HANDICAP

Andrew Toney took me when I was 25 years old to play at Cobb's Creek Golf Club in Philadelphia, Pennsylvania.

FIRST INTRODUCTION TO GOLF

Saucon Valley Country Club in Pennsylvania.

FAVORITE COURSE(S)

I have played with a lot of great players and friends, such as Tiger Woods and Phil Mickelson, and although I really appreciate how great they are at golf, they are pros. I don't take golf that seriously; there are lots of other serious things going on in the world. Golf is a diversion for me. I play for peace with friends. It gives me a reason to spend time with them.

BEST GOLF MEMORIES

CHARLES BARKLEY

HOW DOES GOLF COMPARE TO BASKETBALL	I don't really compare it. I enjoy golf because it gives me downtime; I can get away from things and reality.
ONE GOLF TIP	Don't take golf seriously unless it is your job.
ONE LIFE TIP	Live your truth.
FAVORITE CHARITY GOLF EVENTS	American Century Championship in Tahoe for the scenery; it is a beautiful place (www.tahoecelebritygolf.com).
DREAM FOURSOME	Nelson Mandela, Muhammad Ali, Martin Luther King Jr.
FAVORITE 19TH HOLE DRINK	After golf I like a beer or a vodka.
FAVORITE COUNTRY CLUB GRILL ROOM / 19TH HOLE	I don't really have a favorite.
HOLE IN ONE	I have never made a hole in one.

CHARLES BARKLEY

Courtesy of Pepin Liria

Pepin Liria
BULL FIGHTING

José "Pepin" Liria Fernández is a Spanish bullfighter who has participated in more than seven hundred festivals.

Four.

HANDICAP

My father-in-law from my former wife lived in a golf community, and he took me out to play. This was about fifteen years ago and I was bit by the golf bug right away, but I was at the height of my bullfighting career. In 2008 I retired, and then I really started to play more and work on getting my handicap down. The golf world is great; I can play until I am old, and I do not think about going back to bullfighting.

FIRST INTRODUCTION TO GOLF

I have been very lucky to be invited to play in many great clubs. It's also lucky that many of these people from the golf world are passionate aficionados of bullfighting. Valderrama and San Roque Club are my favorite golf courses. Also La Manga Club in Murcia.

FAVORITE COURSE(S)

BEST GOLF MEMORIES	Because of my position as a bullfighter, I have been fortunate to play in some great Pro-Am events and meet and play with some amazing professional golfers, including Sergio Garcia, Seve Ballesteros, Luke Donald, and Miguel Jimenez, who has become a good friend. In 2011, Miguel Jimenez invited me to caddy for him at the par 3 contest at Augusta National. That is my best golf memory.
HOW DOES GOLF COMPARE TO BULLFIGHTING	They have some things that are very similar, such as the touch, rhythm that you need, the ritual, and passion. Both bullfighters and golfers are very superstitious with the color of the clothes they use for tournaments or bullfights. In both, you need patience that must be learned. In both, you must be very aware of the location of your body, the rhythm, and movements. The character of the person who does well is the same; they must work hard, be methodical, and sacrifice. They both live for their profession. The danger is different! Also the reward is different. If you do well and kill the bull in the correct or the best way, you cut off the ear as a reward.

Enrique Ponce, El Fandi, and Jose Maria Manzanares all play golf because I introduced them to it. |
| ONE GOLF TIP | Play the game. Go and try it at any age, and enjoy it. I wish I was introduced to the game of golf at a young age. I was introduced to bullfighting and I did very well, so who knows what would have happened if I were introduced to golf at a young age? |
| ONE LIFE TIP | Have humility. Golf is a great teacher for humility. Appreciate family—family is very important. |

I play in almost every charity golf tournament that invites me. If I can lend my image to help others, I am happy to do it. Oncología Infantil de Murcia—Children with Cancer (www.afacmur.org).

Seve Ballesteros, José María Olazábal, Miguel Jimenez.

I do not really drink alcohol. I drink water or soft drinks. If I play really well, then I enjoy a good red wine, such as Ribera del Duero.

I have had a very nice time at Valderrama, San Roque, and Club de Campo del Mediterraneo—Sergio Garcia's club.

Yes, I got one at the El Valle Golf Resort in Murcia, Spain. It is a Nicklaus-designed golf course and it was hole number 11, a par 4 that plays to about 286 yards.

Courtesy of Pepin Liria

© Bill Menzel

Jason Kidd
BASKETBALL

Jason Kidd previously played in the NBA as a point guard and is now the head coach of the Brooklyn Nets. A ten-time NBA All-Star, Kidd played for four different teams.

Eight. **HANDICAP**

A high school teammate got me involved in golf, and the high school basketball coach was also the coach of golf. I thought golf would be easy compared to basketball; the ball does not move. This was not true; golf is much harder than I thought.

FIRST INTRODUCTION TO GOLF

Cypress Point Club.

FAVORITE COURSE(S)

Playing golf with President Clinton is my best golfing memory, and when I get to the green in 2.

BEST GOLF MEMORIES

HOW DOES GOLF COMPARE TO BASKETBALL	There is definitely a similarity between basketball and golf as to the mental aspect of the game. With both sports there is a big element of tempo and rhythm.
ONE GOLF TIP	Swing slow and keep your head down.
ONE LIFE TIP	Enjoy your time here; we only have a short time.
FAVORITE CHARITY GOLF EVENTS	The American Century Championship in Tahoe (www.tahoecelebritygolf.com).
DREAM FOURSOME	Bill Gates, President Clinton, and Phil Mickelson. Or Derek Jeter, Tiger Woods, and Jack Nicklaus.
FAVORITE 19TH HOLE DRINK	Water.
FAVORITE COUNTRY CLUB GRILL ROOM / 19TH HOLE	Due Process, the barn clubhouse.
HOLE IN ONE	No.

JASON KIDD

Rubens Barrichello

Rubens Barrichello
FORMULA ONE

Rubens Barrichello, from Brazil, is a racing driver. Barrichello is the tenth highest points scorer in the history of Formula One.

11.2.

HANDICAP

My father-in-law plays golf. He gave me my first set of clubs and we went to the driving range. I fell in love with golf straight away—with the technique and how concentrated you have to be. I love the feeling of hitting the ball on the sweet spot; it is something special. My goal now is to aim for a single-digit handicap.

FIRST INTRODUCTION TO GOLF

Guariroba Golf Club in Sao Paulo, Brazil; Bay Hill and Grand Cypress Golf Club in Orlando, Florida; and in Bali, where I would golf between races. I have played in Japan, China, and Korea. I took my clubs and played everywhere when I was racing.

FAVORITE COURSE(S)

BEST GOLF MEMORIES

I fell in love with golf, and I wanted to meet Tiger Woods. I was able to do so last year at his house. We have a friend in common, and he wanted to know how I trained. We talked in the kitchen and there was a putter there; he said, "Be careful—that one has won many majors."

It was great—I went to one of his training facilities, an analysis center, and got tips.

HOW DOES GOLF COMPARE TO RACING

In golf you put a putt in to become a champ, and in racing you put a lap together to become a champ. Golf is different—you are getting to know people and in nature. It is not like you have 4:28 to finish like in racing. You can play faster or slower. I love a flowing day of golf. With golf, you have a lot of time to think in between shots. Sometimes that can be a bad thing when you hit a bad shot—you have to forget. In racing there is not a lot of time to think.

ONE GOLF TIP

Simple technique equals playing well.

ONE LIFE TIP

Enjoy what you do. Enjoy your time. Give respect and get respect back.

FAVORITE CHARITY GOLF EVENTS

I played in the AT&T Pebble Beach Pro-Am two times along with pro golfers and that was great. I also have a charity in Brazil— the Instituto Barrichello Kanaan—we help kids learn life through sports, and golf will be on the agenda (www.ibk.org.br).

DREAM FOURSOME

Tiger Woods and my two sons, Eduardo and Fernando; they like to drive the golf cart.

When I am with my friends at the clubhouse, I enjoy a glass of red wine, such as California Napa reds.

I really liked the bar and lodge at Pebble Beach, all the people you meet after you play, and the bagpiper who comes out at the end of each day.

No, but close.

Courtesy of Rubens Barrichello

Courtesy of Tahoecelebritygolf.com

John Elway

FOOTBALL

John Elway played his full professional career with the Denver Broncos. Upon retirement in 1999, he had tallied the most victories by a starting quarterback. Elway, who won two Super Bowls, was inducted into the Hall of Fame in 2004.

One.	**HANDICAP**
When I was in college at Stanford, some buddies took me out when I was 18 or 19 years old.	**FIRST INTRODUCTION TO GOLF**
Augusta National.	**FAVORITE COURSE(S)**
My best memory golfing was hitting a 64 at Cherry Hills Country Club in Colorado.	**BEST GOLF MEMORIES**

HOW DOES GOLF COMPARE TO FOOTBALL	The two are similar in their competitive nature. However, golf is better on your body, tougher on your mind. In golf, the only place you have pins is on the golf green; in football they are in your knees and shoulders.
ONE GOLF TIP	Have patience; the harder you try, the worse it gets.
ONE LIFE TIP	Treat others the way you want to be treated.
FAVORITE CHARITY GOLF EVENTS	I really enjoy the American Century Championship and I had my own golf event for twenty years (www.tahoecelebritygolf.com). Now I am hosting the golf event for the Boys & Girls Club of Denver (www.bgcmd.org). We have raised two million in five years, and we are looking to build a new club in Denver.
DREAM FOURSOME	My dad, Tiger Woods, and Phil Mickelson.
FAVORITE 19TH HOLE DRINK	Dewar's and soda.
FAVORITE COUNTRY CLUB GRILL ROOM / 19TH HOLE	Cherry Hills Country Club Men's Grill and the Castle Pines Golf Club Men's Locker Room.
HOLE IN ONE	I have had three holes in one; the best was the first. I did it on my fortieth birthday at Innisbrook Resort and Golf Club in Orlando. It was an event so the booze was already free; I did not have to buy the clubhouse a round.

JOHN ELWAY

Courtesy of Tahoecelebritygolf.com

Mike Eruzione
ICE HOCKEY

Mike Eruzione is a former ice hockey player and was the captain of the 1980 Winter Olympics US National Team during the Miracle on Ice game.

7.5.	**HANDICAP**
I caddied as a kid at a nine-hole course, the Winthrop Golf Club in Winthrop, Massachusetts. I started playing after the Olympics when I was 26 years old. I wish I had played when I was younger.	**FIRST INTRODUCTION TO GOLF**
Old Head Golf Links in Ireland and Augusta National.	**FAVORITE COURSE(S)**
I was playing in the Tom Dreesen Celebrity Golf Classic with Dan Jansen and John Congemi. I had not practiced, didn't take any swings, and I was hungover, and I got a hole in one.	**BEST GOLF MEMORIES**

HOW DOES GOLF COMPARE TO HOCKEY	The feel and touch and the impact through the puck and through the golf ball are similar. Hockey helped my golf game. The biggest thing for golf is patience. In golf you have to go shot by shot, stroke by stroke, hole by hole.
ONE GOLF TIP	Have fun and enjoy yourself; it is only a game.
ONE LIFE TIP	Have a great work ethic.
FAVORITE CHARITY GOLF EVENTS	Winthrop Foundation, based in my hometown, and the Mario Lemieux Celebrity Invitational (www.mariolemieux.org).
DREAM FOURSOME	Mario Lemieux, Dan Marino, and John Congemi, and we would drink wine and smoke cigars.
FAVORITE 19TH HOLE DRINK	Red wine.
FAVORITE COUNTRY CLUB GRILL ROOM / 19TH HOLE	Ritz Carlton in Jupiter, Florida.
HOLE IN ONE	Six—I won a new car once for a hole in one I got at a tournament in Boston. I can remember shots I hit in Tahoe five years ago, but not my wife's birthday.

MIKE ERUZIONE

© Bryan O'Brien

Pat Jennings
SOCCER

Pat Jennings is a retired soccer goalkeeper from Northern Ireland. He played a record 119 games for the Northern Ireland National Team.

Eight.

HANDICAP

Tottenham Hotspur. I went to Scotland and caddied for the Tottenham players Jimmy Greaves, Bill Brown, Peter Baker.

FIRST INTRODUCTION TO GOLF

Royal County Down Golf Club, Royal Portrush Golf Club, and anywhere in Ireland.

FAVORITE COURSE(S)

It gets me away for three to seven hours. One of my great memories is when I played in the Dunhill Masters with Greg Norman. I also played with John Daly at the Pro-Am at Royal Portrush.

BEST GOLF MEMORIES

HOW DOES GOLF COMPARE TO EUROPEAN FOOTBALL	I earned a living playing football. I would not want to have to earn a living playing golf. It is never a bad day on the golf course.
ONE GOLF TIP	If you enjoy playing golf, keep playing.
ONE LIFE TIP	Keep your good health.
FAVORITE CHARITY GOLF EVENTS	I have a golf event—the Co-operation Ireland Pat Jennings Golf Classic at Royal County Down—that I have been hosting for twenty years (www.cooperationireland.org). The mission of Co-operation Ireland is "to underpin political agreement on the island of Ireland by building positive relationships at community level, both within Northern Ireland and between Northern Ireland and the Republic of Ireland, through the promotion of mutual understanding and co-operation."
DREAM FOURSOME	Frank Carson, Rory McIlroy, and my son.
FAVORITE 19TH HOLE DRINK	Whatever comes up. Whatever is there in front of me.

Some of my best memories are from the Footballers' Classic at La Manga Club in Spain. There are about forty former football players and we play golf for three or four days. Great fun.

No, but I have hit the pin.

© Peter Robinson/EMPICS Sport. Courtesy of Press Association Photos Limited.

© Rodney Burkes

Paul O'Neill
BASEBALL

Paul O'Neill is a former right fielder and five-time World Series Champion over the course of his seventeen-year career. He was also a five-time All-Star.

Six.	**HANDICAP**
After baseball, Andy Pettitte and Roger Clemens played, and I went with them.	**FIRST INTRODUCTION TO GOLF**
Shadow Creek, Muirfield Village Golf Club, and Trump International in Palm Beach.	**FAVORITE COURSE(S)**
I was first in an event for the club championship at Trump International.	**BEST GOLF MEMORIES**

HOW DOES GOLF COMPARE TO BASEBALL	In both you hit the ball and there is a long swing. Baseball can get in the way of golf.
ONE GOLF TIP	Learn to hit irons, especially the pitching wedge.
ONE LIFE TIP	Live your days. Don't get too down, as good things are always in the future. It is hard to believe as we get older that the future is going to be better than the past, but it's true.
FAVORITE CHARITY GOLF EVENTS	Michael Jordan's Celebrity Invitational Tournament and my charity, Right Field Charities (www.mjcigolf.com and www.pauloneill21.com/rfc/).
DREAM FOURSOME	Tiger Woods, Jack Nicklaus, and Arnold Palmer.
FAVORITE 19TH HOLE DRINK	I enjoy red wine, such as cabernet from Napa Valley.
FAVORITE COUNTRY CLUB GRILL ROOM / 19TH HOLE	Trump International has the prettiest clubhouse.
HOLE IN ONE	I have had three, but the one I just got at Shadow Creek was the first one I ever got in a tournament.

*We had already arranged that I would interview Paul after his round while he was playing in the Michael Jordan Celebrity Golf Tournament. He had just made a hole in one on 17.

WELCOME TO THE 67th ANNUAL OLD-TIMERS' DAY!

PAUL O'NEILL

Courtesy of Tahoecelebritygolf.com

Emmitt Smith
FOOTBALL

Emmitt Smith is a retired running back who played in the NFL for fifteen seasons. After being chosen in the first round of the draft, Smith played for the Dallas Cowboys and Arizona Cardinals.

Twelve.

HANDICAP

College buddies asked me to go, and I tagged along.

FIRST INTRODUCTION TO GOLF

Augusta National.

FAVORITE COURSE(S)

Golfing with Payne Stewart the year before he died, at the Bob Hope Tournament at PGA West.

BEST GOLF MEMORIES

HOW DOES GOLF COMPARE TO FOOTBALL	Both involve mental toughness and focus for four hours long. I think golf is mentally and emotionally difficult.
ONE GOLF TIP	Patience.
ONE LIFE TIP	Proper attitude, positivity, and good friends.
FAVORITE CHARITY GOLF EVENTS	The American Century in Tahoe and AT&T are my favorite events to play in; and I host my own charity event, The Emmitt Smith Celebrity Invitational (www.tahoecelebritygolf.com, www.attpbgolf.com, and www.emmittsmith.com/celebrity-invitational).
DREAM FOURSOME	Tiger Woods, Michael Jordan, and my dad.
FAVORITE 19TH HOLE DRINK	Tequila Herradura.
FAVORITE COUNTRY CLUB GRILL ROOM / 19TH HOLE	Any 19th hole.
HOLE IN ONE	Not yet.

EMMITT SMITH

Courtesy of Tahoecelebritygolf.com

Shane Battier
BASKETBALL

Shane Battier is a two-time NBA champion who currently plays for the Miami Heat. He previously played for two other NBA teams, as well as the US National Team.

Eighteen.

HANDICAP

When I was 12, I was a caddy in Birmingham, Michigan.

FIRST INTRODUCTION TO GOLF

My favorites are the Inverness Country Club in Chelsea, Michigan and Oakland Hills Country Club in Michigan.

FAVORITE COURSE(S)

I am living them now at Edgewood Country Club. Also, playing in the American Century Championship and getting a birdie on 17.

BEST GOLF MEMORIES

HOW DOES GOLF COMPARE TO BASKETBALL

In golf and basketball, you are not going to make every shot; you will have errors. Don't let bad shots get you out of whack.

ONE GOLF TIP

Practice your short game.

ONE LIFE TIP

Do well, do good. Help others.

FAVORITE CHARITY GOLF EVENTS

The Tahoe American Century Championship; it is the highlight of my summer (www.tahoecelebritygolf.com).

DREAM FOURSOME

My dad, Tiger Woods, and Jim Gaffigan.

FAVORITE 19TH HOLE DRINK

Ice cold Budweiser.

FAVORITE COUNTRY CLUB GRILL ROOM / 19TH HOLE

The bar at my house is my favorite 19th hole—the Goat Bar—it is the patron animal.

HOLE IN ONE

No, I have not gotten a hole in one yet.

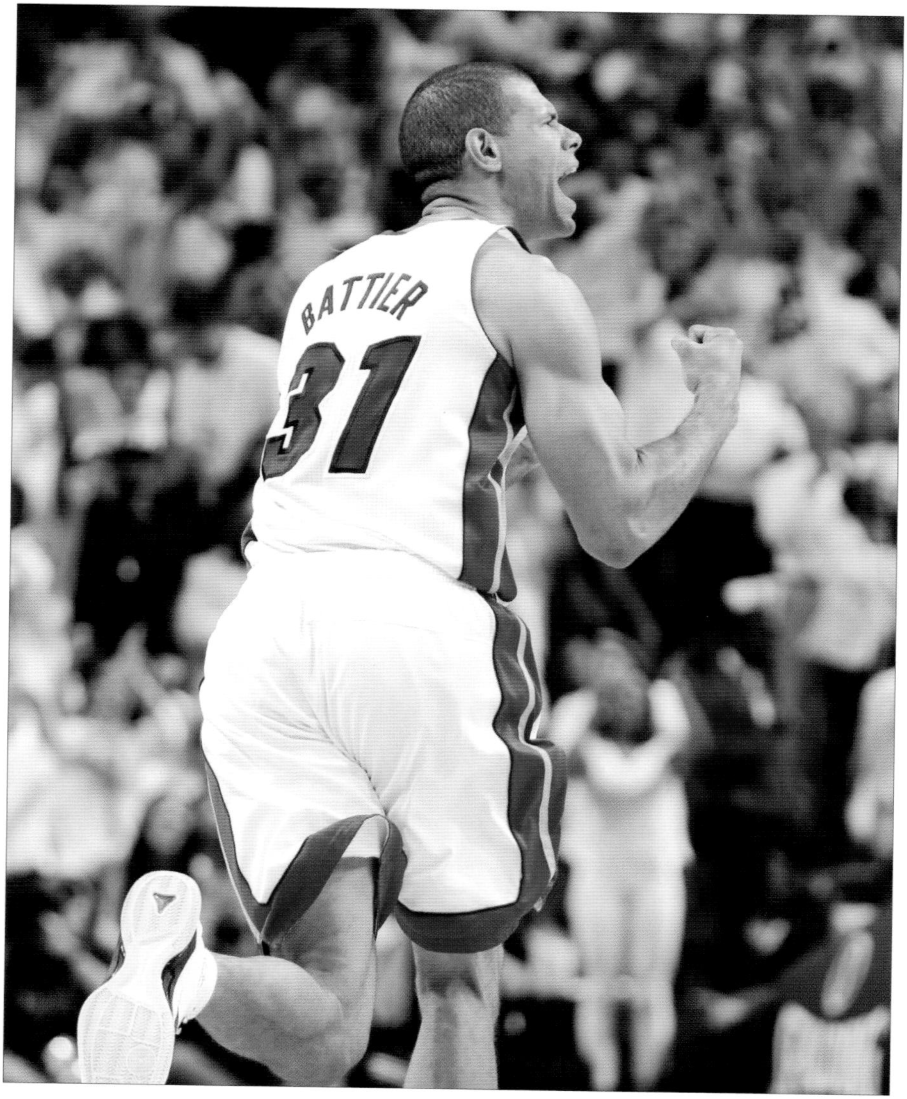

© AP Photo/Lynne Sladky

© AP Photo/Gill Allen

James Tomkins
ROWING

James Tomkins is an Australian rower and seven-time World Champion. He has participated in the Olympics six times and has won three gold medals and one bronze. He has also won two Rowing World Cups.

Four.

HANDICAP

Both my parents played. We lived in a little country town in Victoria, Australia, and I would go with them. We played nine holes on Sunday afternoon. Then I played now and again during university.

FIRST INTRODUCTION TO GOLF

Royal Melbourne Golf Club and Kingston Heath Golf Club. Royal Melbourne Golf Club is a thirty-six-hole golf club in Australia, located in Black Rock, Victoria, a suburb of Melbourne. It is the pinnacle of golf in Australia, its courses being the oldest and most well-renowned in the country. Barnbougle Dunes in Tasmania, Australia is a really amazing golf course, as well.

FAVORITE COURSE(S)

BEST GOLF MEMORIES	Playing Cape Kidnappers in New Zealand with my daughter, who was 9 at the time. She was driving the cart and I was walking, and we were all alone out on this beautiful course. The setting was very beautiful and I had my own caddy.
HOW DOES GOLF COMPARE TO ROWING	Before the 1996 Summer Olympic Games in Atlanta, the entire rowing team was staying in Blairsville, a suburb of Atlanta, and the Butternut Creek Golf Course was across the street. We would all go and play nine holes and it helped us completely get our minds off the Olympic Games, rowing, racing—it was a complete break. In rowing, I have the personal challenge of constantly wanting to improve, be better and win, and that is where golf lends itself perfectly to this. For me, it is also a bit of fun with my mates.
ONE GOLF TIP	Set up right; if you do, you are 90 percent of the way to a good shot. Try and hole every shot.
ONE LIFE TIP	Play more golf. The sport is great because it has self-regulation. Great sport mimics life—sometimes you play well and score badly and sometimes you play badly and score well.
FAVORITE CHARITY GOLF EVENTS	I support Pat Rafter's charity and the charities that support breast cancer and ovarian cancer (http://www.makeitpossible.com/ambassadors/pat-rafter-on-factory-farming.php).
DREAM FOURSOME	Tiger Woods, Michael Jordan, Barack Obama, and Greg Norman.
FAVORITE 19TH HOLE DRINK	Right after I get off the golf course, I like a lemon squash and bitters and, after that, a Carlton draft beer.

Bonville Golf Resort—the deck area over 18th hole. It is a par 5 over water, and it is good fun watching people come in.

Yes, two. One was in a Pro-Am in Queensland and the pro was being interviewed. The other was at the National Golf Club. It was a 195-meter par 3. I used an 8-iron, and it bounced and went in.

Courtesy of James Tomkins

JAMES TOMKINS

Courtesy of Tahoecelebritygolf.com

Marcus Allen
FOOTBALL

Marcus Allen is a former running back for the Los Angeles Raiders and the Kansas City Chiefs. He ran for 12,243 yards over the course of his sixteen-year career.

Seven.

HANDICAP

Friends introduced me to the game of golf when I was in my mid-20s. Guys on the team, I believe they took me to Riviera Country Club—not a bad place to start, I guess.

FIRST INTRODUCTION TO GOLF

I have so many that I like and I have played, but two favorites are St. Andrews and Augusta National.

FAVORITE COURSE(S)

My best memory was at the American Century Championship in Tahoe when I birdied 16, 17, and 18. It was a great feeling. I enjoy golf and that event very much because this is our locker room, the golf course. We challenge ourselves and each other, talk trash, bet, and talk about life, all here on the course and at the event.

BEST GOLF MEMORIES

HOW DOES GOLF COMPARE TO FOOTBALL

In both sports the fundamentals are very important, but more so in golf than football. You need to be fundamentally sound; if you are not taught correctly, it is very hard. I have always been confident, and that helps in both sports. I joke about golf that I know how to win, I just need to learn how to play.

ONE GOLF TIP

Play with your father.

ONE LIFE TIP

Be honest.

FAVORITE CHARITY GOLF EVENTS

The American Century Championship in Tahoe is a great event and my charity event, the Marcus Allen Charity fundraiser (www.tahoecelebritygolf.com).

DREAM FOURSOME

Bill Gates, Larry Ellison, and Warren Buffett.

FAVORITE 19TH HOLE DRINK

Arnold Palmer.

HOLE IN ONE

Yes, I have had one hole in one at a course in Tampa. Derrick Brooks and Eric Dickerson were there, so it was real. It was a par 3 at 230 yards.

© AP Images

MARCUS ALLEN

© AP Photo/Frank Weise

Bruce Jenner
DECATHLON

Bruce Jenner is a former US track and field athlete who won the gold medal for decathlon in the Montreal 1976 Summer Olympics.

Seven.

HANDICAP

I was training for the Olympic Games, and I couldn't do anything where I would get injured, so a friend got me into golf. It is a game you can take up later on in life and actually get better. I played with good players, watched videos, listened, and learned the game on my own. I did not have a lot of lessons. I am not obsessed.

FIRST INTRODUCTION TO GOLF

Sherwood Country Club—there are no tee times. For my fiftieth birthday, I bought a membership at Sherwood. I will go and hit balls for an hour and work on my short game, then play nine holes. Also Casa de Campo—I really enjoyed it when we went there.

FAVORITE COURSE(S)

BEST GOLF MEMORIES   Golfing with my kids and when we are together. I have ten kids and a couple of the boys play—Robert, Brandon, and Brody. I took Kylie and Kendall and they tried it, but it didn't catch on.

HOW DOES GOLF COMPARE TO THE DECATHLON   There is absolutely no correlation between the 400 or the shot put and golf. It is a totally different game. Aggression was good in my sport. Golf is the opposite—you cannot get excited. You almost need to take a valium before you go out and play golf. There is a challenging aspect; not just skill—you need patience, good kinesthetic, and good touch and feel helps.

ONE GOLF TIP   You need lots of patience and work on your short game—practice. Everyone makes mistakes; it comes down to who recovers the best and makes the least amount of mistakes.

ONE LIFE TIP   Enjoy the ride. Enjoy every day, and steal every moment of happiness.

FAVORITE CHARITY GOLF EVENTS   The Drew Brees Celebrity Championship is a great event in San Diego. It is stroke play, so it becomes very competitive.

DREAM FOURSOME   Phil Mickelson, Ian Poulter, and Bubba Watson.

FAVORITE 19TH HOLE DRINK   Gatorade and popcorn.

FAVORITE COUNTRY CLUB GRILL ROOM / 19TH HOLE   I was playing in the Callaway Golf Foundation charity event at Riviera Country Club and they had a contest on the driving range. You had to hit out 185 yards, out to a junk car. I used a 6-iron and, in

TWO GOOD ROUNDS SUPERSTARS

one shot, hit the car. I called my wife, who was always complaining that I played in all these golf tournaments and said, "I am calling you and fulfilling one of my fantasies." She said, "Bruce, what are you talking about?" I told her I was fulfilling the fantasy to call and tell her I won a car at a golf tournament. She paused and did not say congratulations or that it was great. She said, "What type of car?" It was a Mercedes C350. (I put an "I love Golf" sticker on the dashboard.) She said, "I really want the S550." So my free car cost me an extra 50k. The funny thing is, she drove it for a while and then we gave it to her mother. After a few months, her mother called us and said, "I went to the Mercedes dealership because the car was too big for me, and they were so nice they traded it for a C300 at no cost." So it was almost the same car I won originally.

No holes in one, but I have had two double eagles.

HOLE IN ONE

© AP Photo

Courtesy of Tahoecelebritygolf.com

Dan Quinn
ICE HOCKEY

Dan Quinn is a former ice hockey player who spent fourteen years in the NHL. Quinn, who's Canadian, is also a professional golfer.

Zero.	**HANDICAP**
My grandfather bought me clubs for my tenth birthday, and I played with my grandfather. I caddied when I was 11 and 12 years old at the Thames Valley Golf Club in Ontario, Canada. I have three brothers and two sisters, and they all play golf. We have a Quinn Open where my uncles, dad, grandfather, and the family all play.	**FIRST INTRODUCTION TO GOLF**
Shinnecock Hills Golf Club and Turnberry Resort in Scotland.	**FAVORITE COURSE(S)**
Playing in Lake Tahoe at the American Century and being a caddy for pro golfers. I retired from pro hockey and caddied for Jesper Parnevik for fun in 2003, and later, in 2009, started caddying for Ernie Els as a business opportunity. Being a caddy is serious, hard work and a lot of fun. At the HSBC, Els came in second and it was the second time I was working for him. The Grand Slam in	**BEST GOLF MEMORIES**

Bermuda was great, and one of the best moments was the Monday practice round at Torrey Pines Golf Course. It was 3 or 4 in the afternoon, and the sun was setting over the Pacific and no one, not even the volunteers, was on the course. Just a caddy and a player with no one around. It was a special walk and a special chat.

HOW DOES GOLF COMPARE TO HOCKEY

The hand-eye coordination. Hockey is fast and reactionary, and golf is slow throughout. In hockey I play left-handed and in golf I play right-handed. A lot of Russian hockey players are right-handed and a lot of Canadian players are left-handed. In hockey, we have the summers off, three to four months, so it was great to play golf.

ONE GOLF TIP

Look forward and don't beat yourself up over shots. Don't look back at shots. Enjoy the game.

ONE LIFE TIP

Look forward in life and golf. I would be better if I followed my own advice.

FAVORITE CHARITY GOLF EVENTS

American Century Celebrity Golf Championship in Lake Tahoe (www.tahoecelebritygolf.com). I have been playing in it for twenty-two years, and it is a blessing. It is a great opportunity for golf enthusiasts, and it raises millions for charity. It is televised nationally.

DREAM FOURSOME

My brother Kevin, Ernie Els, and Bruce Springsteen. If Bruce doesn't play, he can drive the cart just as long as he brings his guitar along.

FAVORITE 19TH HOLE DRINK

Cold Molson Canadian beer.

My favorite is the Bel-Air Country Club in Los Angeles with Ernie Els. The gin table card room off the bar is a card room overlooking the golf course. We have been known to close many 19th holes.

I have had five holes in one. The first one was at the Rolling Hills Country Club in Pittsburgh, Pennsylvania.

FAVORITE COUNTRY CLUB GRILL ROOM / 19TH HOLE

HOLE IN ONE

© AP Photo/Lenny Ignelzi

Courtesy of John Eales

John Eales
RUGBY UNION

John Eales is a former Australian rugby player who won the Rugby World Cup twice. He was nicknamed "Mr. Nobody" because nobody is perfect.

It is a twenty now. In the past I had it down to a twelve.

HANDICAP

A mate of mine lived near a golf course. We would collect golf balls, and his brother took us to play a round. Later, when I was in university, I played a little, but then I turned pro and was playing Rugby Union full time and golf took a backseat.

FIRST INTRODUCTION TO GOLF

The most beautiful golf course in Australia is the Bonville Golf Resort, located halfway between Sydney and Brisbane on the Coffs Coast.

FAVORITE COURSE(S)

In 1999, we were in Europe for seven weeks for the World Cup matches, and we arrived in Dublin and played a round of golf at Portmarnock Golf Club. We had a competition amongst the teammates then drank Guinness. It was a wonderful start to a

BEST GOLF MEMORIES

successful World Cup. The Australian team won both the 1991 and 1999 World Cups.

HOW DOES GOLF COMPARE TO RUGBY UNION

There are a few ways they are similar—with the goal kicking it is just you and the ball, and in golf it is just you and the club. There are a lot of similar principles when playing golf and rugby. You line up, keep your head down, go slow, and follow through to the posts. There is routine no matter what the situation—it can be a six-foot putt or a kick to win a game. Retreat to routine to make it a controlled situation.

ONE GOLF TIP

The last shot doesn't matter. It's the one you are playing now. This is very relevant in sports to be able to concentrate and be in the moment no matter what is happening.

ONE LIFE TIP

Find the joy in what you do, even in routine. Everything we do has its routine moments. If you can find the joy in that, then you are winning. Those able to be in the moment are the more consistently successful.

FAVORITE CHARITY GOLF EVENTS

Sony Foundation Australia has a golf event as part of their charity efforts (www.sonyfoundation.org.au). And the organization contributes to the advancement of the Australian community by assisting youth and fostering their talents.

DREAM FOURSOME

The great thing about golf, even if you are not very good, is that you get to spend a lot of time with someone, so my foursome is chosen for how interesting they are: Jean-Pierre Rives—he is a legend in my sport, rugby, and since retirement has become a sculptor and an artist of much renown...and he loves his golf. Greg Norman—no one has done more for Australian golf than the Great White Shark. Ben Perkins—he was my kicking coach when I played rugby, and he is the most interesting, though at times complicated, person I know. He partly based his goal-kicking advice on what he knew from golf, so he could help me on the way around, as well. Paul Simon—I'd love to know how he wrote so many great songs.

FAVORITE 19TH HOLE DRINK

Really, really cold beer—a Vale Ale.

FAVORITE COUNTRY CLUB GRILL ROOM / 19TH HOLE

Flooded Gums Restaurant at the Bonville Golf Resort is my favorite, and they were just awarded a one-hat restaurant. This is Bonville—it is the first and only golf course or golf resort in Australia to be awarded a prestigious hat. (The "chef's hat" is a food rating quality system similar to Michelin rating.)

HOLE IN ONE

No. But early on the first year I was playing golf, I came within an inch of getting a hole in one and didn't realize how difficult it really is until later.

Literary Lad

John Eales is the author of two books, *Learning From Legends*, a sport version and a business version. The books talk about different legends of Australian sports and Australian business, and the lessons that can be learned from each.

© Bill Menzel

Roger Clemens
BASEBALL

Roger Clemens pitched over the course of twenty-four seasons for four teams, most notably the Boston Red Sox and New York Yankees. Clemens has the third most strikeouts of all time. The Cy Young Award winner was also an eleven-time All-Star.

Six.

HANDICAP

I was at the University of Texas in 1982 and one of my teammates, Mike Capel, played golf and I went out with him. I was really bad, so he gave me three clubs to go off and play and leave him alone. I met Butch Harmon in 1987 in Houston and took a lesson. Two years later, my wife bought me my first set of golf clubs.

FIRST INTRODUCTION TO GOLF

I really enjoy Shadow Hawk Golf Club, The Club at Carlton Woods, and Grand Pines Golf Club.

FAVORITE COURSE(S)

The Plantation Golf Course in Maui, Hawaii is great; the scenery of the bay and village is incredible. Seeing the world through golf is fantastic.

BEST GOLF MEMORIES

HOW DOES GOLF COMPARE TO BASEBALL	Yes, there are some comparisons. The transfer of weight from a pitching standpoint is very much like golf. I have met as many neat people in golf as I have in baseball.
ONE GOLF TIP	Watch the pros really closely—watch them.
ONE LIFE TIP	Even if you fail a lot, don't give up; keep going.
FAVORITE CHARITY GOLF EVENTS	We host golf events for the foundation my wife, Debbie, and I started—the Roger Clemens Foundation—to raise funds to help children (www.rogerclemensfoundation.org). Also, I support the Wounded Warriors and play in golf events that support them (www.woundedwarriorproject.org). The Bob Hope Classic is a great event that supports charities. I have played in the Bob Hope Classic for twenty years and have won two times—once with Carson Daly and Jeff Altman and then with Matthew McConaughey and Mike Eruzione.
DREAM FOURSOME	George H.W. Bush, Christy Mathewson, and Babe Ruth.
FAVORITE 19TH HOLE DRINK	I sip stuff people hand me. I drink an Arnold Palmer. I am a lightweight.
FAVORITE COUNTRY CLUB GRILL ROOM / 19TH HOLE	The grill that overlooks the Plantation Course in Maui on the 18th hole.

TWO GOOD ROUNDS SUPERSTARS

I have made five holes in one and three in competition.

First was at the Bob Hope Chrysler Classic on the second hole; I was with Mike Eruzione and Matthew McConaughey. Another was at Poppy Hills and I was with Billy Andrade and Brad Faxon.

© AP Photo/Willis Glassgow

Courtesy of Tahoecelebritygolf.com

Joe Theismann
FOOTBALL

Joe Theismann is a former NFL quarterback. Theismann was a two-time Pro Bowler for the Washington Redskins and quarterback during the Redskins' Super Bowl XVII victory.

Three.

HANDICAP

I started in golf and became interested because I was a caddy in New Jersey at the Forsgate Country Club. It was different back then than it is now.

FIRST INTRODUCTION TO GOLF

I really like Old Head Golf Links in Ireland and the Robert Trent Jones Golf Club in Lake Manassas, Virginia.

FAVORITE COURSE(S)

My best golf memory actually happened to my father. We were playing with a friend, Joe Walton, and we were on a par 3 and my father was at the tee. He was in the middle of his swing and a big branch fell right near him, almost on him, and he completed his swing unaffected by the branch. He got a hole in one.

BEST GOLF MEMORIES

HOW DOES GOLF COMPARE TO FOOTBALL	Firing of the hips, rotation of the body, tempo, and thinking your way through football—much of the same is true on the golf course. It is a game of percentages, percentage shots, percentage throws, distances—there are four downs in football and four shots on most holes.
ONE GOLF TIP	Go see a pro—take lessons and get started correctly.
ONE LIFE TIP	Don't let other people tell you that you can't do something. Be your own person.
FAVORITE CHARITY GOLF EVENTS	Tampa Encompass and St Jude; any event that supports St. Jude—it is such a great charity (www.b4btampabay.org and www.stjude.org).
DREAM FOURSOME	Two sons and my dad. Or Tiger Woods, Phil Mickelson, and Tom Watson.
FAVORITE 19TH HOLE DRINK	Arnold Palmer after golf. Or Cristal Champagne.
FAVORITE COUNTRY CLUB GRILL ROOM / 19TH HOLE	Tap Room at Pebble Beach.
HOLE IN ONE	No, but I did get an eagle on 18 at Edgewood Golf Course during the American Century Championship in Tahoe. It was in front of a huge crowd on Sunday in the final round. People were going crazy and I ran around the green like Hale Irwin and was giving people high fives.

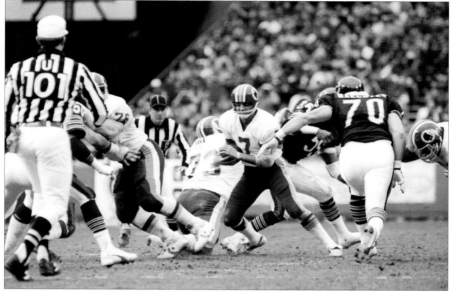

© Associated Press

Theismann and Taylor

When asked if Theismann had ever played golf with Lawrence Taylor, who was involved in the famous play that ended Theismann's career and was featured in the opening scene of *The Blind Side*, his response was, "Yes, we have played golf a couple of times together, definitely in Tahoe, and I won't let him play on my left side."

Courtesy of Tahoecelebritygolf.com

Lawrence Taylor
FOOTBALL

Lawrence "L.T." Taylor is a Hall of Fame football player. Taylor was a linebacker for the New York Giants in the NFL. He won two Super Bowls while playing for the Giants.

Two.

HANDICAP

An agent introduced me to golf years ago when I was with the Giants. He invited me to play. I was in my late 20s. Then I quit and started playing again in 1999.

FIRST INTRODUCTION TO GOLF

Augusta National.

FAVORITE COURSE(S)

My favorite memory of golfing is at the Westchester Open on the Pro-Am day; I made a double eagle.

BEST GOLF MEMORIES

HOW DOES GOLF COMPARE TO FOOTBALL	Football is about aggression and golf can't be aggressive. Golf is calming. That is what I like—it is calm and if you are worried about your golf game and everyone else is concentrating, then you're in trouble.
ONE GOLF TIP	Don't worry about hitting it hard and long. Stay smooth.
ONE LIFE TIP	Hard for me to say. I don't even follow them. There are good days and bad days. As long as you have a pleasant personality, you will always come out on top.
FAVORITE CHARITY GOLF EVENTS	The American Century Celebrity Golf Championship in Lake Tahoe (www.tahoecelebritygolf.com).
DREAM FOURSOME	Barack Obama, Bill Clinton, and Beyoncé Knowles.
FAVORITE 19TH HOLE DRINK	Chivas on the rocks.
FAVORITE COUNTRY CLUB GRILL ROOM / 19TH HOLE	I like the Kinloch Golf Club in Richmond, Virginia. I can hang out with all the guys, have a good time, and smoke cigars. Also, the Ridge at Back Brook is great—the bartenders and people make it well worth it.
HOLE IN ONE	I have had eight or nine.

LAWRENCE TAYLOR

OZZIE
SMITH

© Elisa Gaudet

Ozzie Smith
BASEBALL

Ozzie Smith is a former shortstop who played for two teams in the MLB for almost twenty years. The league-leading shortstop for career assists and doubles was inducted into the Baseball Hall of Fame in 2002.

Six.	**HANDICAP**
They needed a celebrity to hit balls at manager Whitey Herzog's golf tournament in St. Louis. I was instantly hooked.	**FIRST INTRODUCTION TO GOLF**
Sage Valley Golf Club and Boone Valley Golf Club, my home course.	**FAVORITE COURSE(S)**
My best memory is shooting 68 then 69 at Fox Run, my two best rounds.	**BEST GOLF MEMORIES**

HOW DOES GOLF COMPARE TO BASEBALL	The hand-eye coordination is similar. Also, being able to take what you learn and do on the practice range or field and bring it to the golf course or field. The key to success is transferring the range to the course. Consistency—it is the same in both sports. The challenge is to be consistent. Golf is work and it fills the competitive void. I love to compete and work for that, and golf presents that challenge.
ONE GOLF TIP	Before anything, alignment is important. Line up and minimize the area of your mistakes.
ONE LIFE TIP	You only get out what you put in.
FAVORITE CHARITY GOLF EVENTS	I am the president of the Gateway PGA Foundation. We are taking organizations and helping them to continue with the PGA REACH (Recreation, Education, Awareness, Community, and Health, www.gatewaypga.org/pgareach). Bellerive Country Club in St. Louis will play host to the 2013 Senior PGA Championship. We hope to show other cities what they can do to work in community outreach.
DREAM FOURSOME	Fred Couples, Tiger Woods, Jack Nicklaus, Gary Player.
FAVORITE 19TH HOLE DRINK	Michelob Ultra.

I really enjoy the camaraderie and people at Boone Valley Golf Club. **FAVORITE COUNTRY CLUB GRILL ROOM / 19TH HOLE**

Not yet. **HOLE IN ONE**

© AP Photo/Mary Butkus

© AP Photo/Rusty Kennedy

Ronnie Lott
FOOTBALL

Ronnie Lott is a football player who played cornerback, free safety, and strong safety for four professional football teams. Lott was inducted into the Pro Football Hall of Fame in 2000.

Seventeen.

HANDICAP

My rookie year, in 1981, kids in the neighborhood took me to Pruneridge Golf Club to play nine holes; then I stopped for fifteen years.

FIRST INTRODUCTION TO GOLF

Spyglass Hill Golf Course at Pebble Beach.

FAVORITE COURSE(S)

Always beating Marcus Allen and Joe Montana.

BEST GOLF MEMORIES

HOW DOES GOLF COMPARE TO FOOTBALL	There is no correlation; in football you have to be angry, and you can't be angry in golf.
ONE GOLF TIP	Play like you are shooting free throws.
ONE LIFE TIP	There are exams in life.
FAVORITE CHARITY GOLF EVENTS	Marcus Allen Celebrity Golf Tournament in Los Angeles. I used to have one at Pebble Beach, but we stopped.
DREAM FOURSOME	Tiger Woods, Barack Obama, Bill Russell, and Jim Brown.
FAVORITE 19TH HOLE DRINK	A mojito.
FAVORITE COUNTRY CLUB GRILL ROOM / 19TH HOLE	Spyglass Hill Golf Course at Pebble Beach.
HOLE IN ONE	No.

RONNIE LOTT

© Mary T. Fouraker

Ron Duguay
ICE HOCKEY

Ron Duguay, from Canada, played twelve seasons in the NHL for four different teams. He currently works as a hockey analyst for MSG.

HANDICAP

Ten.

FIRST INTRODUCTION TO GOLF

I was 17 and with hockey friends in Sudbury, Ontario, Canada. There would be a bunch of pro hockey guys who would play in charity golf events, and when I went I did not enjoy it at first. It was very frustrating, and then I took lessons and began playing with better golfers and playing with the alumni in the New York area.

FAVORITE COURSE(S)

Old Oaks Country Club in Westchester and Idylwylde Golf and Country Club in Canada. Idylwylde is a difficult course around a beautiful lake. It is a love/hate relationship because of the beauty and the frustration.

BEST GOLF MEMORIES

I enjoyed playing in Michael Jordan's charity golf tournament. Also, one of my best golfing memories is playing golf with Ian Baker-Finch. It is the best round I have played with a pro golfer. He was very giving of himself and a nice, classy man.

HOW DOES GOLF COMPARE TO HOCKEY

You have to be athletic and have hand-eye coordination.

ONE GOLF TIP

Stay calm when hitting the ball. Do not muscle through the shots. Have a loose grip with the hands.

ONE LIFE TIP

Be caring and kind to other people.

FAVORITE CHARITY GOLF EVENTS

Michael Jordan's—I played with Dan Jansen and we were three shots behind the leaders (www.mjcigolf.com). It was televised, and we were miked for forty-five minutes. I got a taste and feel for what it would be like to play professional golf, the pressure, adrenaline rush, and the competition. We finished third.

DREAM FOURSOME

Kevin James, Vince Vaughn, and Zach Galifianakis. I really love to laugh, and it would be great to hang with them for five hours.

FAVORITE 19TH HOLE DRINK

Michelob Ultra Light beer does it for me.

The Rangers have an event every September, a preseason outing at Old Oaks in Westchester, and it is great to spend time at the bar with current players and alumni each year.

FAVORITE COUNTRY CLUB GRILL ROOM / 19TH HOLE

No, but close; during a charity event, it was one inch from the hole.

HOLE IN ONE

© AP Photo/Tom Mihalek

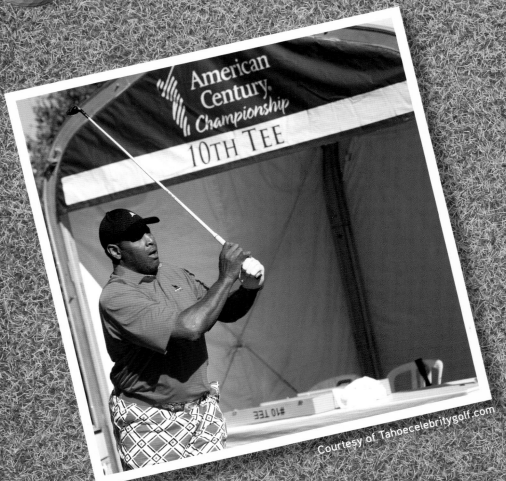

American Century Championship

10TH TEE

#10 TEE

Courtesy of Tahoecelebritygolf.com

Richard Dent
FOOTBALL

Richard Dent, a recent inductee to the Pro Football Hall of Fame, played defensive end, most notably for the Chicago Bears. He was the MVP of Super Bowl XX.

Nine.

HANDICAP

My uncle caddied for Gary Player for fifteen years. I used to hang out with my uncle while he was working as a caddy at Eastlake Golf Club in Atlanta, and that is how I first became interested in golf. I played golf in high school, and it was actually the first sport I played before football. My history teacher was also the golf coach, and you know how history teachers are—they take two days to tell a story, so I became more interested in football.

FIRST
INTRODUCTION
TO GOLF

East Lake Golf Club in Atlanta; it is where I grew up.

FAVORITE
COURSE(S)

BEST GOLF MEMORIES	My best golfing memories are my two holes in one and playing Augusta National three times with Dan Marino and Jim Colbert.
HOW DOES GOLF COMPARE TO FOOTBALL	In football, you need to put yourself in position to make the play and it's the same with golf. If you have bad alignment in football and with golf, you don't get the best results. One difference is in golf you pull the trigger; in football you have a supporting cast.
ONE GOLF TIP	Alignment.
ONE LIFE TIP	Golf is like life—sometimes it is on and working well. Figure out how you can recover quickly. Find the right things you need to be doing.
FAVORITE CHARITY GOLF EVENTS	The Murray Brothers have a great event I go to every year—Murray Bros. Caddyshack Charity Golf Tournament— and my foundation, Make a Dent Foundation (www.murraybrosgolf.com and www.makeadentfoundation.com).
DREAM FOURSOME	Muhammad Ali, Michael Jordan, and Dr. Martin Luther King Jr.
FAVORITE 19TH HOLE DRINK	Vodka with a splash of cranberry, a splash of grapefruit, and a lime.
FAVORITE COUNTRY CLUB GRILL ROOM / 19TH HOLE	The Augusta National Clubhouse.

136   TWO GOOD ROUNDS SUPERSTARS

Two holes in one. There is nothing like the first time.

The first was at the Royal Melbourne Country Club in Chicago. It was the 5th hole, 145 yards, with the wind blowing in my face. I used the 8-iron and it did one hop and it was in.

© AP Photo/David Boe

RICHARD DENT

Courtesy of Tahoecelebritygolf.com

Rick Rhoden
BASEBALL

Rick Rhoden was an MLB pitcher for sixteen years on four different teams. Rhoden now plays professional golf and has qualified for the US Senior Open and played in several Champions Tour events.

Three.

HANDICAP

I grew up in Florida, so I was surrounded by golf courses. My dad introduced me to golf, but he himself did not start playing until he was in his mid-30s. I went a few times with him when I was a kid, but it was not until I started playing baseball and signed my contracts that I had money and went out and bought clubs and golf shoes. I was 18 when I got clubs and started playing.

FIRST INTRODUCTION TO GOLF

I really like Pebble Beach, and the Edgewood Tahoe Golf Course is the best for scenery; they are both such beautiful places. I played a lot at a course called Pablo Creek Golf Club in Jacksonville, Florida. It is a really nice Tom Fazio-designed course that was in the top one hundred courses for a while.

FAVORITE COURSE(S)

BEST GOLF MEMORIES

In 1991 when I won the American Century event in Tahoe. I was really scared; I got a birdie on the last hole, which put me in the playoffs with Bill Laimbeer. He ended up shooting four consecutive shots into the pond in front of the green on the par-5 18th hole. I had a birdie and won. They named the pond Lake Laimbeer as a result.

HOW DOES GOLF COMPARE TO BASEBALL

Pitching in baseball and golf both have a lot of similarities, such as the transfer of weight. Not every shot is a good one, and not every pitch is a good one. It is the culmination of shots or pitches that makes a great athlete. Also, you have to have a short memory for both. If I give up a home run in baseball or hit a hazard in golf, I have to forget it right away and focus on the next shot or pitch. I cannot let it affect me.

ONE GOLF TIP

Don't hit in the air. Hit into the ground.

ONE LIFE TIP

Life is like golf—you need patience. Also, golf is great because you spend time with friends and family, and you can play it at any age. You can play until you can't walk.

FAVORITE CHARITY GOLF EVENTS

My favorite is the Tahoe American Century event because it is so beautiful and I have won the event eight times (www.tahoecelebritygolf .com). I have played in probably five hundred charity golf events and they are all good when they are helping and giving back. My favorites are the ones that help children. Mario Lemieux has a great event (www .mariolemieux.org). The Shriners Hospital also has a special place in my heart (www.shrinershospitalsforchildren.org). I went to a Shriners Hospital two times when I was a kid. I hurt my leg and they really helped me out. I started playing sports at 14 and this was prior to that, so who knows, maybe if it was not for them I would not have played sports.

Arnold Palmer, Jack Nicklaus, and Babe Ruth.

I really enjoy wine, and the owners of BR Cohn Winery are good friends. Every year after the tournament, my wife and I go to their winery for a few days. I also enjoy a Crown Royal and vodka.

The Resort at Pelican Hill on the coast of Newport Beach in Southern California has an amazing view from their clubhouse.

Eleven holes in one. Probably my favorite is the one I made while playing in the US Senior Open at the NCR Country Club in Kettering, Ohio. I have played in thirty-five professional Champion Tour events, including four US Senior Open events and two Senior PGA Championship events. Golf is a great equalizer—there is no Air Jordan out here, it is just Michael.

Courtesy of Tahoecelebritygolf.com

© AP Photo/Ed Betz

Clark Gillies
ICE HOCKEY

Clark Gillies, a former ice hockey player, is a four-time Stanley Cup Champion. He played for the New York Islanders and is a member of the Hockey Hall of Fame.

Four.   **HANDICAP**

In 1974, I was playing pro hockey with the Islanders, and I started   **FIRST**
playing in charity events. I play hockey left-handed and play golf   **INTRODUCTION**
right-handed   **TO GOLF**

Meadow Brook Club.   **FAVORITE**
                                                             COURSE(S)

I played on the Celebrity Golf Classic golf tour, and Pierre Larouche   **BEST GOLF**
and I won the two-man event in Ocean City.   **MEMORIES**

HOW DOES GOLF COMPARE TO HOCKEY They are similar in the mental toughness you need to succeed. Jack Wagner and I were playing in the final day of a tournament, and I think he wanted to get under my skin. He asked if I had ever played in the last group on the final day. My response was, "No, but I won four Stanley Cups."

ONE GOLF TIP Don't drink too much coffee before you play golf. Stay steady.

ONE LIFE TIP You can't live a perfect day unless you help someone who does not have to help you.

FAVORITE CHARITY GOLF EVENTS I have a foundation, the Clark Gillies Foundation, and we host the Clark Gillies Celebrity Classic golf tournament (www.clarkgillies .org). The foundation has raised funds and built a pediatric center and a preschool for children with cancer.

DREAM FOURSOME Tiger Woods, Ernie Els, and Bubba Watson.

FAVORITE 19TH HOLE DRINK Bacardi and Diet Coke.

FAVORITE COUNTRY CLUB GRILL ROOM / 19TH HOLE The men's grill room at the Medalist Golf Club, MGD.

HOLE IN ONE I have had three holes in one. The first I never saw; the second was 180 yards at the Huntington Crescent Club.

© Scott Erickson

Scott Erickson
BASEBALL

Scott Erickson is a retired pitcher who played for the Minnesota Twins, Baltimore Orioles, New York Mets, Texas Rangers, Los Angeles Dodgers, and New York Yankees. He threw a no-hitter against the Milwaukee Brewers on April 27, 1994.

Eleven.

HANDICAP

I started working at Cherry Chase Golf Club in Sunnyvale, California, watering the course in junior high. I would get to play for free, and I used to play with my dad's old set of golf clubs that were in the garage.

FIRST INTRODUCTION TO GOLF

Spyglass Hill Golf Course at Pebble Beach and Tralee Golf Course in Ireland.

FAVORITE COURSE(S)

I was playing in a Baltimore Orioles tournament at Waverly Woods Golf Club and on a 180-yard par 3, I got a hole in one using an 8-iron. I won a golf bag.

BEST GOLF MEMORIES

HOW DOES GOLF COMPARE TO BASEBALL	Baseball helped my golf swing. As a pitcher, you are repeating the same pitch. It is the same in golf—you are repeating the same golf swing.
ONE GOLF TIP	Stay back and stay balanced.
ONE LIFE TIP	Enjoy it while you can.
FAVORITE CHARITY GOLF EVENTS	Wounded Warriors, Make a Wish kids charity tournament, and the American Century Celebrity Golf Championship in Lake Tahoe are fun to play (www.woundedwarriorproject.org, www.wish.org, and www.tahoecelebritygolf.com).
DREAM FOURSOME	Elvis, John Wayne, and Babe Ruth.
FAVORITE 19TH HOLE DRINK	Coors Light.
FAVORITE COUNTRY CLUB GRILL ROOM / 19TH HOLE	I like the bar at the Edgewood Tahoe Golf Course. I like the scenery, the beer, and to look at Lake Tahoe and watch the sun go down.
HOLE IN ONE	I have had two. One was at the World Series of Golf, an event made up of all baseball players and friends. I hit a shot 122 yards with a 52-degree wedge and it went in. There were 400 golfers, so I was off the hook for buying drinks. Another time, I was playing with Bret Saberhagen, Phil Nevin, and J.T. Snow, and Nevin hit a shot

that went up through trees and did a backspin into the hole. People were screaming behind the pin on the green. It was embarrassing because when we got there, 40 percent of the ball was leaning over the cup, but it did not go in.

© AP Photo/Linda Kaye

Jeremy Roenick
ICE HOCKEY

Jeremy Roenick is a former NHL player who played for several teams, including the Chicago Blackhawks, Phoenix Coyotes, Philadelphia Flyers, Los Angeles Kings, and San Jose Sharks over the course of his eighteen-season NHL career. He was also part of Team USA in international tournaments.

One.

HANDICAP

Both my parents are golfers, and I would tag along with five or six golf clubs in my hands and pick up how to play the game by playing with them.

FIRST INTRODUCTION TO GOLF

Augusta National, Pebble Beach, Pine Valley, Kingsbarns in Scotland, and Shadow Creek.

FAVORITE COURSE(S)

Competing in the American Century Celebrity Golf Championship in Tahoe. I love to compete and bring all my buddies to Tahoe; it is fun and I enjoy the parties. Also, a trip to Scotland I did with friends.

BEST GOLF MEMORIES

HOW DOES GOLF COMPARE TO HOCKEY

Golf does not help hockey at all. Hockey is high pain levels and you have to be mean. Hockey does help golf in that in golf you need balance, and the slap shot is similar to the golf shot. The hand grip is different, but body rotation and being flexible help in both.

ONE GOLF TIP

Keep your head still. Until you learn to rotate around your head, you are in for a long round.

ONE LIFE TIP

My mom and dad always said, "Treat people the way you want to be treated and you are guaranteed to have a few friends."

FAVORITE CHARITY GOLF EVENTS

Special Kids Network Annual Celebrity Golf Tournament (www .specialkidsnetwork.org). Special Kids Network is an independent nonprofit organization that was created to provide funding for programs that help children and young adults with special needs.

DREAM FOURSOME

Arnold Palmer; Ronald Reagan, he would be fun and he liked to golf; and Jack Nicholson, to make me laugh.

FAVORITE 19TH HOLE DRINK

Vodka soda with a splash of cranberry. And a cold Bud Light, especially on a hot day after a round of golf. Nothing tastes better.

FAVORITE COUNTRY CLUB GRILL ROOM / 19TH HOLE

Pebble Beach Lodge in the barroom after a round. Also I enjoyed the club at Porcupine Creek in Rancho Mirage, California, a very private course that Tim Blixseth built.

I bought a golf course four years ago, the Pembroke Country Club in Pembroke, Massachusetts. I got it out of foreclosure and brought it back to life. It is a fun public track that we revitalized and made affordable for people to play. I grew up playing this course, and it was a good way to save the golf course.

HOLE IN ONE

I have had three. One was on the 17th hole at Whisper Rock. Another time I was playing with some guys, and as I got up to the tee, my partner said, "Scotch and water." I used a 9-iron and knocked it in the hole. There were many Scotches after that. Another time was on my own course. We were playing a tiebreaker hole and I dropped in the hole from 60 yards.

Courtesy of Jeremy Roenick

Courtesy of Tahoecelebritygolf.com

Kevin Millar
BASEBALL

Kevin Millar is a former MLB first baseman who played for four different teams. Millar was an integral part of the Red Sox's trip to the 2003 American League Championship Series and the 2004 World Series.

Seven.

HANDICAP

My dad took me to play golf when I was 12 or 13, and then I was just involved in baseball and stopped. I regret I did not play more golf while I was still playing baseball and take advantage of the perks.

FIRST INTRODUCTION TO GOLF

Pebble Beach and Shadow Creek.

FAVORITE COURSE(S)

I got an eagle at Pebble Beach on a par 5. Also, playing at the Tahoe event, the American Century; it is always a great time.

BEST GOLF MEMORIES

HOW DOES GOLF COMPARE TO BASEBALL	The hand-eye coordination and mental aspects are similar. You have to deal with a lot of failure in both sports.
ONE GOLF TIP	Watch the ball.
ONE LIFE TIP	Only God can judge you. To dare is to do and to fear is to fail.
FAVORITE CHARITY GOLF EVENTS	The Children's Miracle Network (www.classic.childrensmiraclenetworkhospitals.org).
DREAM FOURSOME	Rory, for his golf swing; Shaq, for his comedy; and JLo, for her looks.
FAVORITE 19TH HOLE DRINK	Jack Daniels and Diet Coke.
FAVORITE COUNTRY CLUB GRILL ROOM / 19TH HOLE	The Whisper Rock Golf Club in Scottsdale, Arizona.
HOLE IN ONE	No.

KEVIN MILLAR

© Karen & Dan Jansen

Dan Jansen
SPEED SKATING

Dan Jansen is a retired speed skater who won a gold medal for the United States in world record time during the 1994 Olympics.

Four.	**HANDICAP**
I grew up in Wisconsin, and my Dad taught me—I have played ever since I can remember. I probably started at 8 years old and would go out with him once a week during the summer. I loved it but started skating, and that took over.	**FIRST INTRODUCTION TO GOLF**
Augusta National—it is everything it is made out to be and more. I also like Whistling Straights and the River course at Blackwolf Run.	**FAVORITE COURSE(S)**
Getting a golf lesson from Karen Palacios. She was a David Leadbetter golf instructor at Lake Nona in Florida. Four years later, we met up again at a Gary Player outing and started dating. Nine months later, we were married.	**BEST GOLF MEMORIES**

HOW DOES GOLF COMPARE TO SPEED SKATING

The individual nature of the two sports is similar. I love that about both skating and golf—you have to rely on yourself. You are blamed when it is bad, but also get the credit when it is good.

ONE GOLF TIP

Ninety-nine percent of us do not play golf for a living, so have fun and just enjoy the game.

ONE LIFE TIP

Try to learn something from every situation, both the good and the bad.

FAVORITE CHARITY GOLF EVENTS

I really enjoy playing in the American Century Celebrity Championship in Tahoe and the Michael Jordan Tournament (www.tahoecelebritygolf.com and www.mjcigolf.com).

I also have my own foundation, the Dan Jansen Foundation (www.djfoundation.org). The mission of the foundation is to solicit financial support and distribute funds to charities with an emphasis on the fight against leukemia, which is what took the life of my sister Jane. The foundation also supports youth sports programs, and educational and scholarship awards.

DREAM FOURSOME

Jack Nicklaus, Arnold Palmer, and Tiger Woods. Tiger is the best player to play the game in my lifetime and very influential to the game of golf. Jack was the same whether he won or lost; always gracious. He would win and lose with the same amount of dignity. Arnold was amazing with the fans and his appreciation of the game. He is very accommodating and always signing autographs. Something I always wonder about is how Arnold does it; he never says no.

I enjoy a cold beer after golfing and sometimes a gin and tonic.

I enjoy the grill room at Trump National in Charlotte, North Carolina, which is my home course. I enjoy the camaraderie and sitting with my golf buddies after a round, and we reminisce about our golf shots and playing.

I have had five. I am now tied with my wife, Karen. The first one I ever got was at the Tahoe Celebrity event. It was on the 5th hole and it flew right in the cup.

© AP Photo/Thomas Kienzle

DAN JANSEN

Courtesy of Tahoecelebritygolf.com

Greg Maddux

BASEBALL

Greg Maddux is a retired MLB pitcher. He won the Cy Young Award four consecutive years, from 1992 to 1995, and was the first player in league history to do so. He has captured eighteen Gold Gloves, the most in league history.

Four.	**HANDICAP**
My dad and my brother taught me when I was 18 or 19 years old. My dad was in the Air Force, so I learned on the Air force base.	**FIRST INTRODUCTION TO GOLF**
Pine Valley—I like everything about it.	**FAVORITE COURSE(S)**
Playing at Pebble Beach with my brother and some friends.	**BEST GOLF MEMORIES**

HOW DOES GOLF COMPARE TO BASEBALL	I think golf and baseball are totally different; golf is much harder. What I liked about golf is it helped me get away from baseball and get a break from baseball, but still spend time and play in tournaments with teammates.
ONE GOLF TIP	Play every chance you get. If you break a club, take a day off.
ONE LIFE TIP	Treat people the way you want to be treated.
FAVORITE CHARITY GOLF EVENTS	The Greg Maddux Celebrity Invitational in Las Vegas (www.maddux31.com).
DREAM FOURSOME	Dad, my brother, and my son.
FAVORITE 19TH HOLE DRINK	A bottle of red wine. I am not picky; I prefer ones from Napa Valley, California.
FAVORITE COUNTRY CLUB GRILL ROOM / 19TH HOLE	The lodge at Pebble Beach is my favorite.
HOLE IN ONE	I have had three holes in one. The most memorable was at Spanish Trail Country Club on the 3rd hole. I used a 6-iron and hit it off the toe 172 yards.

© AP Photo/Ric Feld

GREG MADDUX

Ahmad Rashad
FOOTBALL

Ahmad Rashad is a former NFL running back and wide receiver drafted by the St. Louis Cardinals. He then played for the Buffalo Bills and the Minnesota Vikings.

Three.

HANDICAP

Two people introduced me. Bill Murray, one of my best friends, bought me clubs, and Michael Jordan took me out ten years ago and was patient. I started and stopped for a while. It takes a lot of patience, but I got to a single-digit handicap after a year when I focused on it. It takes patience and time. Once the golf bug gets you, you are hooked.

FIRST INTRODUCTION TO GOLF

The Bears Club, Sebonack Golf Club, and Eugene Country Club.

FAVORITE COURSE(S)

One day I had three eagles and a birdie in one round, and I shot an 84. Golf is a wonderful life sport that brings people together who do not run in the same circles or walks of life. It is a beautiful game where people get to spend time together.

BEST GOLF MEMORIES

HOW DOES GOLF COMPARE TO FOOTBALL

I don't think any sport translates. Golf is not a sport where you can tell by looking at the guy how good he is. If you have been a pro athlete, you are able to concentrate, and that is a major part of all sports, especially golf.

ONE GOLF TIP

Lower your expectations, and enjoy the scenery and locations when you play.

ONE LIFE TIP

There is always another shot, always another shot—life is like that.

FAVORITE CHARITY GOLF EVENTS

Ahmad Rashad Golf Classic to benefit White Plains Hospital at Quaker Ridge Golf Club and the Michael Jordan Celebrity Invitational Golf Tournament ARIA at Shadow Creek in Las Vegas (www.ahmadrashadgolfclassic.org and www.mjcigolf.com). Also, I host the Ahmad Rashad Celebrity Classic to benefit the REACH Foundation at Mohegan Sun in Connecticut (www.ahmadrashadcelebrityclassic.com).

DREAM FOURSOME

Michael Jordan, Sidney Poitier, Tiger Woods, and Arnold Palmer.

FAVORITE 19TH HOLE DRINK

Diet Coke.

FAVORITE COUNTRY CLUB GRILL ROOM / 19TH HOLE

Clubhouse at the Bears Club. There, you can run into anyone, and you can trash talk. Tour players play there, so I can run into Rory McIlroy, Ernie Els, and Keegan Bradley.

I have had two. One was when I was playing with Tiger Woods and Rory McIlroy, which is what makes this an amazing game. The funny thing is we are hacks, amateur golfers, the pressure is on them, not me; they are supposed to be the best in the world. I am more proud of my three eagles in one day than the two holes in one.

© AP Photo/Kathy Willens

Courtesy of Tahoecelebritygolf.com

Brett Hull
ICE HOCKEY

Brett Hull is a Canadian-American former NHL player. He played for five different teams from 1986 to 2005. He won the Stanley Cup with both the Dallas Stars and the Detroit Red Wings.

Zero.	**HANDICAP**
My freshman year of college, a few buddies were going and I asked them if I could go along. The first time I played was at the Enger Park Golf Course in Duluth, Minnesota.	**FIRST INTRODUCTION TO GOLF**
Augusta National.	**FAVORITE COURSE(S)**
My first hole in one was my best memory. It was at the Nemadji Golf Course in Superior, Wisconsin. I used an 8-iron and hit it 153 yards.	**BEST GOLF MEMORIES**

HOW DOES GOLF COMPARE TO HOCKEY	The technique is different. In hockey we slide through our shots; you can't do that in golf. I think hockey hurts the golf swing.
ONE GOLF TIP	Tempo.
ONE LIFE TIP	Be a good person.
FAVORITE CHARITY GOLF EVENTS	My favorites that I like to play in are the American Century in Tahoe, Mario Lemieux's event, and Michael Jordan's (www.tahoecelebritygolf.com, www.mariolemieux.org, and www.mjcigolf.com). It is great to hang out with all these athletes and be able to play golf with them.
DREAM FOURSOME	Jack Nicklaus, Jesus—I am not religious, but I would like to pick his brain about what is going on now—and Tiger Woods.
FAVORITE 19TH HOLE DRINK	Tequila Sunrise made with grapefruit juice.
FAVORITE COUNTRY CLUB GRILL ROOM / 19TH HOLE	The Tap Room at Pebble Beach.
HOLE IN ONE	I have had eight.

BRETT HULL

© Elisa Gaudet

Ed Reed
FOOTBALL

Ed Reed is an NFL free safety who played for about a decade with the Ravens before signing with the Houston Texans in 2013.

Around a seventeen. I shoot in the high 80s to low 90s.

HANDICAP

My high school physical education teacher would make circles on the ground and we had plastic balls we would practice hitting. In college, I went with some teammates and hit at the range, and then I rented clubs and played nine holes.

FIRST INTRODUCTION TO GOLF

The Biltmore Golf Course in Miami and Canongate Golf Club in Georgia.

FAVORITE COURSE(S)

During off-season, I was making more birdies and I shot an 82; that is my lowest round.

BEST GOLF MEMORIES

Dreams come true. I just played in my first Pro-Am at the Honda Classic with Tiger Woods and Matt Kuchar.

HOW DOES GOLF COMPARE TO FOOTBALL	For both, it is about the seven inches between your ears. Golf has made me more focused and patient with myself and other people. Even playing on a team, being mentally more patient helps. I see guys struggling out there and they come back; it is inspiring. There are peaks and valleys.
ONE GOLF TIP	Practice and repetition.
ONE LIFE TIP	Keep doing the reps and keep getting up when life knocks you down. Play one hole at a time and one game at a time.
FAVORITE CHARITY GOLF EVENTS	Anquan Boldin Celebrity Golf Classic that supports Q81 Foundation and the Jonathan Ogden Celebrity Golf Classic (www.Q81.org and www.jonathanogdenfoundation.org).
DREAM FOURSOME	Tiger Woods, Obama, Michael Jordan, and my dad, Edward.
FAVORITE 19TH HOLE DRINK	Cold beer.
FAVORITE COUNTRY CLUB GRILL ROOM / 19TH HOLE	Capital Grill in Buckhead, Atlanta, Georgia.
HOLE IN ONE	No hole in one, but birdies are coming.

ED REED

© AP Photo/Gene Puskar

Denny Hamlin
NASCAR

Denny Hamlin is a race car driver in the Sprint Cup Series and the Nationwide Series.

HANDICAP

One. Last year I was a twenty-three, so I am working hard on my game.

FIRST INTRODUCTION TO GOLF

In racing, a lot of the team guys would go play golf on Saturdays. They invited me along, and I got started in 2004, when I was 23.

FAVORITE COURSE(S)

The Kinloch Golf Club in Richmond, Virginia.

BEST GOLF MEMORIES

Golfing with Bubba Watson in Phoenix, Arizona in 2010. It was just Bubba and me, and our managers had arranged it. He is a great guy, and we have become friends. As a result, I caddied for Bubba at the Par 3 Contest at the Masters in 2012. Augusta National is amazing; everything is perfect.

DENNY HAMLIN

HOW DOES GOLF COMPARE TO RACING

It is not about being the best. That does not guarantee you will win, even if you are the fastest or hit it the furthest. In both sports, it is about the mental part and physics. They differ in the fact that with racing you have a team, a car, and the driver—lots of moving parts—which is different from golf.

ONE GOLF TIP

Keep your head down.

ONE LIFE TIP

Live every day in the moment. A buddy of mine, Greg Fornelli, who also caddied for me at the American Century Championship, has fought cancer three times. I see him, and he is always in a good mood and positive; he lives every day in the moment and I really admire that.

FAVORITE CHARITY GOLF EVENTS

The American Century Championship in Tahoe (www.tahoecelebritygolf.com). It is the greatest experience golfing. I feel like a PGA Tour pro. The event is set up perfectly, a real first-class event. Also, I have the Denny Hamlin Foundation, which is dedicated to raising awareness and funds for children with cystic fibrosis (www.dennyhamlinfoundation.org/).

DREAM FOURSOME

Bubba Watson, Tiger Woods, and Ricky Fowler.

FAVORITE 19TH HOLE DRINK

Jack and Coke.

TWO GOOD ROUNDS SUPERSTARS

The Tap Room at Pebble Beach.

FAVORITE COUNTRY CLUB GRILL ROOM / 19TH HOLE

I have had one, and I am very lucky. It was at the Peninsula Club on Lake Norman, North Carolina on the 7th hole, 129 yards.

HOLE IN ONE

© Bill Menzel

DENNY HAMLIN

© Bonnie Blair

Bonnie Blair
SPEED SKATING

Bonnie Blair is a former speed skater who skated for the United States in four Olympics, tallying five medals.

Seventeen or eighteen.

HANDICAP

My parents played and signed me up for junior golf when I was 10 years old, but I did not enjoy it then. After the 1988 Olympic Games, I was invited to play in charity golf tournaments, and most of those were a scramble format. I started to enjoy it and playing other events where I would play my own ball. Then I just enjoyed playing myself beyond the charity events and kept playing. I appreciated golf more the second time around.

FIRST INTRODUCTION TO GOLF

Bay Course at Kapalua in Hawaii, The Challenge at Manele on the Island of Lanai in Hawaii, Merrill Hills Country Club in Waukesha in Wisconsin, and Lincoln Center Fields.

FAVORITE COURSE(S)

I played in the Western Open Pro-Am at Cog Hill in 1994. It was a skins game, and there were a number of notable golfers and athletes playing, such as Peter Jacobsen, Lee Trevino, Nick Price,

BEST GOLF MEMORIES

and Walter Payton. I was very nervous, as I was used to scramble events and this was skins, where we had to hit every other shot with our partner. I was partnered with Tiger Woods, and this was early in his career. We got to the 18th hole and all the skins were on the table, so we all had to do a shootout. We did a chip off to see who won the skins. We had to hit over a bunker to a slanted green. Everyone went and they were hitting high shots in the air, and they were landing off the green or rolling off. I just gunned it, and it ended up eight feet from the pin. So we won the skins and won the whole thing. I really enjoyed getting to meet all those people, and they were all really nice guys. Later that year I was named Sportsman of the Year by *Sports Illustrated*, which was interesting, as I really thought it was going to be Nick Price.

One of the best rounds I have ever had was when I was more than eight months pregnant. I am not sure if it was the extra weight I could put behind my shots or if it slowed down my swing.

HOW DOES GOLF COMPARE TO SPEED SKATING

Both sports are very individualistic. I am competing against myself. In both, you need to focus. However, I did sprints in skating—it was a shorter amount of time; you need to focus a lot longer for golf. In both sports, you have to be able to pick yourself up and go back at it, and get back into it even after adversity or failing.

ONE GOLF TIP

Take a lesson so you don't develop bad habits; they are hard to break.

Find things that you thoroughly love and enjoy, that you are passionate about. You will not always have a good day, and the passion and love will help you get back into it.

ONE LIFE TIP

The Vince Lombardi Golf Classic is my favorite; it has been running for forty-three years (www.lombardifoundation.org). I was the first female to ever play in the event and the only one to ever play pregnant. I played pregnant two times; once I was eight months along.

FAVORITE CHARITY GOLF EVENTS

Michael Jordan, Annika Sorenstam, Mario Lemieux.

DREAM FOURSOME

Miller Genuine Draft.

FAVORITE 19TH HOLE DRINK

Merrill Hills Country Club in Waukesha, Wisconsin—my home course, where I live now. That is my favorite place and Mark, the bartender there at the club, is great.

FAVORITE COUNTRY CLUB GRILL ROOM / 19TH HOLE

No, but I witnessed my husband make one and my dad make one when I was younger. For both it was their only hole in one, so if things happen in threes then I should make one before I leave this earth.

HOLE IN ONE

© Bill Menzel

Gary Sheffield

BASEBALL

Sheffield is a retired MLB player. He played predominantly as an outfielder with eight teams from 1988 to 2009—the Milwaukee Brewers, San Diego Padres, Florida Marlins, Los Angeles Dodgers, Atlanta Braves, New York Yankees, Detroit Tigers, and the New York Mets.

Fourteen.

HANDICAP

In 2009 I retired and stared playing golf. I hit a shot three hundred yards down the middle of the fairway, and I was hooked from that point.

FIRST INTRODUCTION TO GOLF

Old Memorial Golf Club in Tampa, Florida. There is lots of water on the course and it is very challenging.

FAVORITE COURSE(S)

The first game I played in 1999, at Old Memorial.

BEST GOLF MEMORIES

HOW DOES GOLF COMPARE TO BASEBALL	When I step on the field, whatever is going on, I forget about it and focus on baseball. The same with golf; I just focus on golf when I play.
ONE GOLF TIP	Swing easy.
ONE LIFE TIP	Enjoy life to the fullest; tomorrow is not a promise.
FAVORITE CHARITY GOLF EVENTS	Big Daddy Celebrity Golf Classic, Warrick Dunn Celebrity Golf Tournament, Joe Namath March of Dimes Celebrity Golf Classic, and the Tim Tebow Celebrity Golf Tournament (www .bigdaddygolfclassic.com and www.timtebowfoundation.org).
DREAM FOURSOME	Tiger Woods, Michael Jordan, Muhammad Ali, and Mike Tyson driving the cart.
FAVORITE 19TH HOLE DRINK	I like Grand Marnier, but I am drinking more water now.
FAVORITE COUNTRY CLUB GRILL ROOM / 19TH HOLE	Cigar room at Old Memorial. I like to relax and talk to the guys.
HOLE IN ONE	No.

© AP Photo/Lenny Ignelzi

HR 500 Cigars

While many celebrities create signature wines, Gary Sheffield, in collaboration with Rocky Patel, created the HR 500 cigar. Sheffield's appreciation of great cigars translated to a limited-edition release of cigars celebrating his career achievement of hitting 500 home runs.

© John D. Morris

Barry McGuigan
BOXING

Barry McGuigan, a former Irish professional boxer known as The Clones Cyclone, was a World Boxing Association Featherweight Champion.

Eighteen.

HANDICAP

My brother is a scratch golfer and my uncle Dennis is the president of the Clones Golf Club in Ireland. They influenced me a lot. I love the guys that are involved in golf—Padraig Harrington and Paul McGinley.

FIRST INTRODUCTION TO GOLF

Lough Erne Golf Resort in Northern Ireland, the Faldo course; London Golf Club at Brands Hatch; and the Royal St. George's Golf Club in England.

FAVORITE COURSE(S)

On the 3rd hole, a par 3, at Royal Port Rush, I sunk a 30 foot putt. In 1978, I was 17 and training for matches, and I used to run on the 9th fairway of Royal County Down Golf Club. I would run off the beach to the bunkers and do interval training; it was softer on the joints to do it there.

BEST GOLF MEMORIES

HOW DOES GOLF COMPARE TO BOXING	Rotation is key in both.
ONE GOLF TIP	Relax over the ball; do not grip the club too hard.
ONE LIFE TIP	Exercise and stress your heart at least three times per week.
FAVORITE CHARITY GOLF EVENTS	CLIC Sargent—a charity that helps children and young people with leukemia and cancer (www.clicsargent.org.uk). My daughter Danika was diagnosed with leukemia at age 11. She recovered and is now an actress. We are very active in helping this organization and families.
DREAM FOURSOME	Halle Berry, Mark Twain, Gary Player.
FAVORITE 19TH HOLE DRINK	Uisce as Gaeilge, which means "water from Ireland" in Gaelic.
FAVORITE COUNTRY CLUB GRILL ROOM / 19TH HOLE	Albany Golf Club.
HOLE IN ONE	No, but my son did when we were playing at Boughton Golf Club in Kent, England.

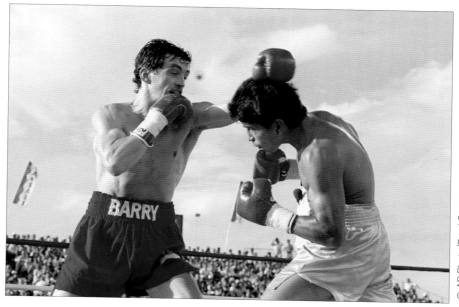

BARRY MCGUIGAN

© Bill Menzel

Tony Romo
FOOTBALL

Tony Romo is the current quarterback for the Dallas Cowboys.

Zero.	**HANDICAP**
My dad taught me to golf when I was 12 in the backyard.	**FIRST INTRODUCTION TO GOLF**
My favorite course is Meadowbrook Country Club in Wisconsin.	**FAVORITE COURSE(S)**
My best memories golfing were with my dad when I was learning to play the game and spending time with him.	**BEST GOLF MEMORIES**

HOW DOES GOLF COMPARE TO FOOTBALL	The big similarity is being able to come back after a negative play or a bad shot.
ONE GOLF TIP	Get a good grip.
ONE LIFE TIP	Pray.
FAVORITE CHARITY GOLF EVENTS	American Century Championship in Tahoe and the Youth for Christ Foundation (www.tahoecelebritygolf.com and www.yfc.net).
DREAM FOURSOME	Dad, my wife Candice, and my brother-in-law Chace.
FAVORITE 19TH HOLE DRINK	Gatorade.
FAVORITE COUNTRY CLUB GRILL ROOM / 19TH HOLE	The Tap Room at Pebble Beach.
HOLE IN ONE	Not yet.

TONY ROMO

© Rodney Burkes

Ken Griffey Jr.
BASEBALL

Ken Griffey Jr. is a retired baseball outfielder who played for three different MLB teams. Griffey is known for his prolific home-run-hitting ability. He was a member of thirteen All-Star teams.

Six.

HANDICAP

My dad introduced me to golf. I would hang out with him when I was 7 years old and we would see how far we could hit the golf ball.

FIRST INTRODUCTION TO GOLF

Pebble Beach, Isleworth Golf & Country Club, and Stone Canyon Golf Club.

FAVORITE COURSE(S)

I played eighteen with Jack Nicklaus at the AT&T Pebble Beach event. I was more nervous than anything else in my pro career. I parred the first hole.

BEST GOLF MEMORIES

HOW DOES GOLF COMPARE TO BASEBALL	They are two different swings; the planes and the stance are different.
ONE GOLF TIP	Lots of chipping.
ONE LIFE TIP	Play this game forever with friends and family.
FAVORITE CHARITY GOLF EVENTS	Michael Jordan's event is great (www.mjcigolf.com). And the Ken Griffey Jr. Family Foundation.
DREAM FOURSOME	Tiger Woods, Jack Nicklaus, Arnold Palmer, and Gary Player. I don't even have to play; I can just watch.
FAVORITE 19TH HOLE DRINK	Lemonade.
FAVORITE COUNTRY CLUB GRILL ROOM / 19TH HOLE	Home, at my place.
HOLE IN ONE	Yes, I have one from the Disney's Palm Golf at the Walt Disney World Resort. I used a 5-iron and hit 195 yards.

KEN GRIFFEY JR.

© Scott Hamilton

Scott Hamilton
FIGURE SKATING

Scott Hamilton is an American figure skater who captured four consecutive US Championships and four consecutive World Championships, in the years 1981 to 1984, and a gold medal in the 1984 Olympics.

Now an 11.7, but it has been down to a 6.

HANDICAP

A friend in Denver introduced me to golf when I was 25. I have had nine brain surgeries and a shoulder surgery, and I would play golf once a week when I was recuperating; I wanted to be outside.

FIRST INTRODUCTION TO GOLF

The Golf Club of Tennessee.

FAVORITE COURSE(S)

I was playing at Sun Valley with a friend, Steven, and we were trying to sabotage each other. I was going to break 80 if I made par on the 18th hole, and I missed the putt. I don't play to be competitive—it is not an extension of my competitive nature—I play to be social and be with friends. When I come back from golf my wife asks me how

BEST GOLF MEMORIES

I played, and I tell her there were no surprises. I enjoy being with friends, their company, and the outdoors. It is an escape.

HOW DOES GOLF COMPARE TO SKATING

They are opposite—skating is aerobic, uses your full body, and is indoors; and golf is outdoors. They both rely on balance. I did incorporate golf into my skating routine. When I did *Stars on Ice,* I had a routine—*Double Bogey Blues*—it was a lot of fun. As part of the routine, I had a remote that would shoot a putter out of the golf bag while I was on ice.

ONE GOLF TIP

Swing the club and take the ball out of the equation, and everything takes care of itself.

ONE LIFE TIP

The key to happiness in life and golf is to lower your expectations.

FAVORITE CHARITY GOLF EVENTS

I really enjoy Vince Gills' event—I played with Johnny Miller and learned a lot—the Vinny Pro-Celebrity Invitational Golf Tournament (www.vincegill.com).

DREAM FOURSOME

Arnold Palmer, Sam Snead, Freddy Couples, and me.

FAVORITE 19TH HOLE DRINK

Root beer float or an Arnold Palmer.

Sherwood Country Club's locker room. It's great to people watch. I was playing once and helping a friend. I was not thinking about the game and ended up winning skins—eight hundred dollars.

FAVORITE COUNTRY CLUB GRILL ROOM / 19TH HOLE

Close, but no.

HOLE IN ONE

Courtesy of Scott Hamilton

Bode Miller
SKIING

Bode Miller is an alpine ski racer with the US Ski Team who has won the gold medal at the Olympics, as well as the World Cup championship, which he has won twice. He has thirty-three World Cup wins.

I don't have one.

HANDICAP

My grandmother took me out to play in New Hampshire when I was about 19.

FIRST INTRODUCTION TO GOLF

My favorite course is Aviara Golf Club in California.

FAVORITE COURSE(S)

Golfing in Hawaii. I actually had a dream that I changed my grip in the middle of playing a golf tournament, that I rotated my wrist. I went out the next day and shot a 73. That was real, not in my dream. I used the rotation I dreamed about and it worked, but just for like one day.

BEST GOLF MEMORIES

HOW DOES GOLF COMPARE TO SKIING
They are both outside, and the actual time you are hitting a golf ball and the actual time you are swinging a club adds up to just a few minutes per round. Skiing is also very short. You need mental focus in both. Skiing is very physical and you can really hurt yourself; golf not so much—you can maybe pull a muscle.

ONE GOLF TIP
Remove stress—people act like they should be really good and get upset when they are not. People should just enjoy playing and play to their personal peak for fun.

ONE LIFE TIP
Remove stress.

FAVORITE CHARITY GOLF EVENTS
Turtle Ridge Foundation is a nonprofit organization supporting adaptive and youth sports programs (www.turtleridgefoundation.org). My favorite event is the Turtle Ridge Foundation Golf & Tennis Tournament and Charity Event.

DREAM FOURSOME
Michelle Wie, Tiger Woods, and Jack Nicklaus.

FAVORITE 19TH HOLE DRINK
Blueberry vodka, soda, and lemonade—it is called an Island Girl.

FAVORITE COUNTRY CLUB GRILL ROOM / 19TH HOLE
My favorite is at Sugarloaf; there is a bar there called The Bag.

HOLE IN ONE
No—I am saving my luck for other more important things.

BODE MILLER

Garrett Gomez
THOROUGHBRED JOCKEY

Garrett Gomez is an American thoroughbred jockey who broke the stakes victories record in 2007.

Four.

HANDICAP

When I was 20 years old, in 1992. Other jockeys invited me a lot of the time, and as I got a little older I started playing. A number of jockeys play golf, including Corey Nakatani, who shoots around a 67 or 68 in a round.

FIRST INTRODUCTION TO GOLF

Manhattan Woods—a buddy is a member; it is beautiful, quaint, with pristine greens that roll like carpet, and you can see downtown Manhattan from the clubhouse. I also like Bethpage Black. I really enjoy good golf courses, different architecture, and the beauty around it.

FAVORITE COURSE(S)

I enjoy playing and striving to get better and the ability to get away from the horses and that life—I don't think about racing for a while. In Chicago, I played fifty-four holes in one day during the summer. It is so difficult to be good at hitting with the same golf club. You can

BEST GOLF MEMORIES

hit with a club one hundred times, and it is never the same hit. Golf is very frustrating and hard, but I enjoy the challenge.

HOW DOES GOLF COMPARE TO HORSE RACING

The conditions will never be the same and never set up the same—not in horse racing and not in golf. For both, you need a lot of concentration; one is fast, one is slow. The two balance each other. In a horse race, your blood is racing. Golf is very calming, and it is completely different than what I am used to.

ONE GOLF TIP

Swing smooth. Don't try to kill the ball.

ONE LIFE TIP

Life is too short; make every day count.

FAVORITE CHARITY GOLF EVENTS

I cohost the Del Mar Charity Classic at the Lomas Santa Fe Country Club that benefits the Winners Foundation, a nonprofit organization established to provide guidance to workers and family members of California's horse racing community facing alcohol or drug related challenges (www.birdeasepro.com/DelMarCharityClassic and www.winnersfoundation.org).

DREAM FOURSOME

Tiger Woods, Michael Jordan, and my wife.

FAVORITE 19TH HOLE DRINK

Diet Coke.

FAVORITE COUNTRY CLUB GRILL ROOM / 19TH HOLE

A great 19th hole memory was after the Del Mar Charity Classic last year. We had a banquet and a book signing for my book, *The Garrett Gomez Story: A Jockey's Journey Through Addiction &*

Salvation, and it was a heartfelt moment for me to give back to the Winners Foundation and the people who have helped me and been there for me.

No.

HOLE IN ONE

© Rodney Burkes

Julius "Dr. J" Erving
BASKETBALL

Julius Erving was a member of three championship teams and is one of the top ten scorers in ABA and NBA history. He was voted Most Valuable Player in both the American Basketball Association and the National Basketball Association, for a total of four MVP awards.

I don't have one, but if I did, it would be a floating thirteen.

HANDICAP

I was in Philadelphia playing with the 76ers, and Dr. Stanley Lorber took me to his club. I got interested in golf, created a few other relationships, and then got hooked. The first time I ever played in a Pro-Am, I was invited by Roger Maltbie and Spalding put clubs together for me.

FIRST INTRODUCTION TO GOLF

I really like Shadow Creek. I am friendly with Steve Wynn and remember when he was building the course with Tom Fazio in 1989. I saw the desert transform into this beautiful place.

FAVORITE COURSE(S)

BEST GOLF MEMORIES	Playing in the Bob Hope Classic with Fuzzy Zoeller.
HOW DOES GOLF COMPARE TO BASKETBALL	It is fundamental to practice and focus. Putting and free throws are similar; however putting is harder. If you make 50 percent of your putts, you are the best in the world. There are still good players in the NBA who are not good at free throws—Shaq and all the ones that make less than 50 percent.
ONE GOLF TIP	Keep your head down. Every time you look up, all you will see is a bad shot. If you are peeping, you come out of your posture.
ONE LIFE TIP	If you don't want people to find out about something, you probably shouldn't do it. Pass on things that you might want to do.
FAVORITE CHARITY GOLF EVENTS	I have been playing in Michael Jordan's tournament for more than ten years, the Marcus Allen Celebrity Charity Golf Tournament, and the Salvation Army Athletes Against Drugs (www.mjcigolf.com). Another cause that is important to me is the fight to cure lupus. My brother Marvin died of lupus.
DREAM FOURSOME	Ray Wilson (my high school coach), Bill Russell, and Ben Hogan.
FAVORITE 19TH HOLE DRINK	Crown Royal and ginger ale.
FAVORITE COUNTRY CLUB GRILL ROOM / 19TH HOLE	The Shadow Creek Grill Room; I have been coming since 1989, but I have not had a Rhondarita, the signature drink.

I have had one at the Riverton Country Club in New Jersey. It was
the second par 3 on the course. I used an 8-iron to hit about 146.
It was on September 25, 1989, and I became a member of the
Johnnie Walker Hole-in-One club.

© AP Photo/Ray Stubblebine

Acknowledgements

I would like to wish a deep and heartfelt thank you to the many people who contributed in some way to this book, especially the athletes who shared their stories and their love of golf. And to the many agents, assistants, friends, and family who helped facilitate the interviews and were a constant support and source of encouragement, especially Pete Falcone, Allan Cooper, Phil Cotton, Bill Corsa, Johnny Rhodes, Diane Durante, Lisa Guerrero, Stacey Williams, Richard Salgado, Bob Broderick, Scott Garwood, Javier Reviriego, Julie Craven, Karen Palacios-Jansen, Dan Lazarek, Bob Fette, BDK Setai Pool Bar & Masters group. A special thank you to the outstanding staff and people who put on two of the best golf tournaments that highlight many of these athletes: the American Century Celebrity Golf Championship and the Michael Jordan Celebrity Invitational.

Photographers Rodney Burkes, Bill Menzel, and John Angelillo, and TahoeCelebrityGolf.com, you are the best!

Charities Supported

Ernie Els – Els for Autism, www.elsforautism.com

Michael Phelps – www.michaelphelpsfoundation.org

Ray Allen – www.ray34.com

Andy Roddick – www.arfoundation.org

Wayne Gretzky – www.mjcigolf.com

Michael Strahan – Hosts the Michael Strahan Charity Golf
    Tournament

Dale Jarrett – Ned Jarrett American Cancer Society Golf Classic

Brandi Chastain – www.reachupworld.com, www.bawsi.org,
    www.mjcigolf.com, www.tahoecelebritygolf.com

Kelly Slater – www.attpbgolf.com

Jerry Bailey – www.pdjf.org

Steve Waugh – www.stevewaughfoundation.com.au

John Smoltz– www.tahoecelebritygolf.com, www.choa.org,
    www.kingsridgecs.org

Oscar De La Hoya – www.goldenboypromotions.com

Charles Barkley – www.tahoecelebritygolf.com

Pepin Liria – www.afacmur.org

Jason Kidd – www.tahoecelebritygolf.com

Rubens Barrichello – www.ibk.org.br

John Elway – www.tahoecelebritygolf.com, www.bgcmd.org

Mike Eruzione –The Winthrop Foundation, www.mariolemieux.org

Pat Jennings – www.cooperationireland.org

Paul O'Neill – www.mjcigolf.com, www.pauloneill21.com/rfc

Emmitt Smith – www.tahoecelebritygolf.com, www.attpbgolf.com,
www.emmittsmith.com/celebrity-invitational

Shane Battier – www.tahoecelebritygolf.com

James Tomkins – Pat Rafter's charity and the charities that
support breast cancer and ovarian cancer

Marcus Allen – www.tahoecelebritygolf.com and the Marcus Allen
Charity Fundraiser

Bruce Jenner – Drew Brees Celebrity Championship

Dan Quinn – www.tahoecelebritygolf.com

John Eales – www.sonyfoundation.org.au

Roger Clemens – www.rogerclemensfoundation.org,
www.woundedwarriorproject.org

Joe Theismann – www.b4tampabay.org, www.stjude.org

Lawrence Taylor – www.tahoecelebritygolf.com

Ozzie Smith – www.gatewaypga.org/pgareach

Ronnie Lott – Marcus Allen Celebrity Golf Tournament

Ron Duguay – www.mjcigolf.com

Richard Dent – www.murraybrosgolf.com,
www.makeadentfoundation.com

Rick Rhoden – www.tahoecelebritygolf.com, www.mariolemieux.org,
www.shrinershospitalsforchildren.org

Clark Gillies – www.clarkgillies.org

Scott Erickson – www.woundedwarriorproject.org,
www.wish.org, www.tahoecelebritygolf.com

TWO GOOD ROUNDS SUPERSTARS

Jeremy Roenick – www.specialkidsnetwork.org

Kevin Millar – www.classic.childrensmiraclenetworkhospitals.org

Dan Jansen – www.tahoecelebritygolf.com, www.mjcigolf.com,
www.djfoundation.org

Greg Maddux – www.maddux31.com

Ahmad Rashad – www.ahmadrashadgolfclassic.org,
www.mjcigolf.com, www.ahmadrashadcelebrityclassic.com

Brett Hull – www.tahoecelebritygolf.com, www.mjcigolf.com,
www.mariolemieux.org

Ed Reed – www.Q81.org, www.jonathanogdenfoundation.org

Denny Hamlin – www.tahoecelebritygolf.com,
www.dennyhamlinfoundation.org

Bonnie Blair – www.lombardifoundation.org

Gary Sheffield – www.bigdaddygolfclassic.com,
www.warrickdunn.com, www.broadwayjoe.tv/philanthropy,
www.timtebowfoundation.org

Barry McGuigan – www.clicsargent.org.uk

Tony Romo – www.tahoecelebritygolf.com, www.yfc.net

Ken Griffey Jr. – www.mjcigolf.com, The Ken Griffey Jr. Family
Foundation

Scott Hamilton– www.vincegill.com

Bode Miller– www.turtleridgefoundaton.org

Garrett Gomez – www. birdeasepro.com/DelMarCharityClassic,
www.winnersfoundaton.org

Julius Erving – www.mjcigolf.com, Marcus Allen Celebrity Golf
Tournament, Salvation Army Athletes against Drugs, Fight to
cure Lupus

About the Author

Elisa Gaudet has spent the past several years working in the golf industry in the United States and Latin America. She worked for the PGA Tour and the Tour de las Américas prior to founding Executive Golf International. She has appeared on numerous radio and TV programs and has been a guest speaker on a variety of golf topics. She has written several golf-related articles and her syndicated "On the Lip" column has been running since 2003. In 2011, she launched Two Good

© John Angelillo

Rounds (www.twogoodrounds.com), a golf lifestyle brand with the first endeavor being the book *Two Good Rounds: 19th Hole Stories from the World's Greatest Golfers*. She splits her time between New York City and Florida.